Publisher's Note:

This edition marks a shift in the binding of this series. The first editions were produced with a spiral binding. This has become far more costly than we think it should be, and would price this series beyond what many would think affordable.

In reponse, we have moved to "perfect" binding which is much more cost effective and offers the reader/user of these prayers some options. We have provided a deep "gutter" (the white space at the inside edge of the page) to permit different bindings to be added.

You may take it to your local service bureau (e.g. Kinko's, Copy Max) and ask them to cut off the binding. You may then
- add a spiral binding
- add a plastic comb binding
- have it three-hole drilled for insertion into a binder

The materials included on the covers of the first edition are found on the covers and last page of this one.

The Daily Office
A Book of Hours for Daily Prayer

After the Use of THE ORDER OF SAINT LUKE

for

Lent and the Triduum

Volume II
(Second Edition)

Dwight W. Vogel, O.S.L.
Editor and Compiler

Issued: February 2002

ORDER OF SAINT LUKE PUBLICATIONS
Akron, Ohio

THE DAILY OFFICE
A Book of Hours for Daily Prayer
After the Use of THE ORDER OF SAINT LUKE
Volume II
(Second Edition)

ISBN 1-878009-44-3

Order of Saint Luke Publications
P.O. Box 22279
Akron, Ohio 44302-0079

http://www.Saint-Luke.org

Production Editor: Timothy J. Crouch, O.S.L.

The Order of Saint Luke invites people throughout the church to use these offices. We also solicit comments based upon their use. Please direct all comments or suggestions to the publishing office.

Other Source References

BCP	*The Book of Common Prayer* (New York: The Church Hymnal Corporation, 1979)
BOH	*The Book of Hymns* (Nashville: The United Methodist Publishing House, 1961, 1966)
LBW	*Lutheran Book of Worship* (Minneapolis: Augsburg Publishing House, 1978)
The Hymnal 1982	*The Hymnal 1982 according to the use of The Episcopal Church* (New York: Church Hymnal Corporation, 1985)
UMH	*The United Methodist Hymnal: Book of United Methodist Worship* (Nashville: The United Methodist Publishing House, 1989)

Table of Contents

Preface vii
    Guidance for Use in Community x
    The Liturgical Psalter x
    Thoughts on Daily Office Rubrics xi

Ordinary of the Hours 1
    Evening Prayer (Vespers or Evensong) 2
    Hymn of Light (*Phos Hilaron*) .... Front Cover
    Evening Prayer Canticle (Metrical Form) 2
        Chant Form .... Front Cover
    Canticle of Mary (*Magnificat*) – ICEL text 4
        Chant Form .... Front Cover

    Compline (Night Prayer) 6
        Canticle of Simeon (*Nunc Dimittis*) 11

    Vigil (Mid-Night Matins) 12
        Canticle of Praise to God (*Venite Exultemus*) 12
        Canticle of the Holy Trinity (*Te Deum Laudamus*) 13

    Morning Prayer (*Lauds*) 15
        Canticle of Zechariah (*Benedictus*) – ICEL text 15
        ICET Text .... Back Cover

    Mid-Morning Prayer (*Terce*) 18
    Mid-Day Prayer (*Sext*) 20
    Mid-Afternoon Prayer (*None*) 22

The Great Litany 24

Propers for Special Feasts and Observances 29

    Compline (*for Lent*) 30
    An Office of Readings 35
    February 24: St. Matthias the Apostle 52
    March 2: John Wesley 53
    March 19: St. Joseph 54
    March 25: Solemn Vespers for the Feast of the Annunciation 55
    March 29: Charles Wesley 60

Propers of the Day for Lent 61

Evening Prayer before Ash Wesdesday 62
Ash Wednesday
    Vigil before Ash Wednesday 66
    Morning Prayer for Ash Wednesday 77
    Solemn Vespers for Ash Wednesday 82
Thursdays in Lent
    Morning Prayer 87
    Evening Prayer 90
Fridays in Lent
    Morning Prayer 94
    Evening Prayer 97
Saturdays in Lent
    Morning Prayer 101
    Vigil 105
Sundays in Lent
    Morning Prayer 111
    Evening Prayer 114
Mondays in Lent
    Morning Prayer 118
    Evening Prayer 122
Tuesdays in Lent
    Morning Prayer 126
    Evening Prayer 130
Wednesdays in Lent
    Morning Prayer 135
    Evening Prayer 139

Propers of the Day for Holy Week 145
Vigil before Palm/Passion Sunday 146
Palm/Passion Sunday
    Morning Prayer 151
    Evening Prayer 155
Monday of Holy Week
    Morning Prayer 159
    Evening Prayer 164
Tuesday of Holy Week
    Morning Prayer 168
    Evening Prayer 172
Wednesday of Holy Week
    Morning Prayer 176
    Evening Prayer 180
Thursday of Holy Week
    Morning Prayer 184

Propers of the Triduum 189
Holy Thursday
    Solemn Vespers 190
    Compline 195
    Vigil 199
Good Friday
    Morning Prayer 201
    Prayers of the Hours at the Crucifixion 205
    Evening Prayer 216
    Vigil 219
Holy Saturday
    Morning Prayer 227
    Mid-Morning Prayer 229
    Mid-Day Prayer 230
    Mid-Afternoon Prayer 232

Great Paschal Vigil 235

(Inside) Front Cover
    The *Phos Hilaron*
    Evening Prayer Canticle (Selected from Psalm 141)
    Canticle of Mary (The *Magnificat*; from Luke 1:39-56) - Chant form

Page 248
    A Collect for The Order of Saint Luke
    The Lord's Prayer (Ecumenical Text)
    The "Spirit Prayer"

(Inside) Back Cover
    The *Gloria*
    Canticle of Zechariah (The *Benedictus*; Luke 1:67-79) - ICET text
    Intercessions for The Order of Saint Luke

Preface

The Order of Saint Luke is a religious order dedicated to sacramental and liturgical scholarship, education and practice. While its origins are rooted in the United Methodist Church, its members come from a number of denominations. In 1988, The Order published *The Book of Offices and Services* to provide resources for its members in their commitment to daily prayer. That same year the General Chapter charged the editor of this series with the responsibility of developing additional resources to enable members to fulfill that commitment.

The first volume of this series was published in 1991 and provided resources for Advent, Christmas, Epiphany, and the Baptism of our Lord. The second volume (for Lent and the Triduum) appeared in 1993, and the third (for the Great Fifty Days) was published in 1994. As a result of the trial use of those three volumes, the General Chapter of the Order reviewed work on this project which had appeared up to that point and made two important decisions about future volumes: (1) they should include the text of the psalms and (2) they should include the text of the hymns. The editor was delighted to comply.

Because we had learned a great deal in the preparation and use of the first three volumes, the decision was made to dispense with volumes related to Ordinary Time using the earlier pattern. At the same time, Brother Timothy Crouch, the director of publications for The Order, developed a larger format, utilizing the spiral binding and marker cover which characterized all subsequent volumes in their first printings. The first volumes in this new format were Volume IV-A (Ordinary Time for the summer months) and IV-B (Ordinary Time for fall), published in 1997. The second edition of Volume I (for Advent through the season after Epiphany) was published in 1998. Publication schedules and other responsibilities of the editor made it necessary to move next to the second edition of Volume III (for The Great Fifty Days) published in 2000. As a result, this book (the second edition of Volume II for Lent and the Triduum) is the latest volume to be published. In each volume, corrections and clarifications are made based on The Order's experience in praying the offices provided up to that point. Using the content of later volumes to interpret, clarify and correct earlier volumes is encouraged.

In order to make these works available to the largest number of persons possible, this new format was established with Volume VI. The increasing expense of the special covers and spiral binding raised the cost of each book to a point where they became far too costly for many. In the new style, users may choose a binding method which best suits their use, at a cost much more reasonable than before.

These volumes are supplemented by *For All the Saints*, edited by Clifton F. Guthrie (Volume V), and a book of daily lectionaries prepared by Abbot Mark Stamm (Volume VI).

The purpose of this series of books is to provide resources for "daily prayer." People who pray daily do so in a variety of ways. Our intent is to reclaim the practice of praying the "Daily Office"— a pattern of praise, prayer, scripture and reflection related to the historic "canonical hours"— specified times for focusing our prayer. The title of the series reflects this intent: *The Daily Office: A Book of Hours for Daily Prayer.*

Our work reflects the following guidelines:

1. The Order of Saint Luke, while a religious community, lives most of its life in dispersion. Thus, even in areas of the country where there are active chapters, daily prayer will more often be a "solitary" office than a "corporate" one. The offices of daily prayer must, therefore, be meaningful when used by individual members.

2. However, the Daily Office is an essential expression of community, even when in dispersion. The Daily Office is the prayer of the Church, not "private devotions." Orders for daily prayer must, therefore, engender a sense of community prayer even when prayed alone. It must also be able to provide a significant resource for use when persons come together to pray.

3. Repetition provides for a depth of appropriation not available when constant change takes place; yet the continual repetition of all content can lead to boredom and emptiness. What is "ordinary" and what is "proper" must be kept in a creative balance. The "ordinary" seeks to reflect those parts of the daily office which have stood the test of time. Thus, the use of the traditional canticles and the evening hymn in the ordinary of the offices is maintained, while other parts of the office change from day to day, week to week and holy day to holy day.

4. We have sought to be inclusive in our references to human beings, and to reflect the rich heritage available to us in the naming of our God who is beyond all names. We have followed the pattern established by The Order of Saint Luke in adopting *The Book of Offices and Services* by frequently using a doxological form from the Eastern church: "Glory to the blessed and holy Trinity."

The ordinary includes offices or services for seven of the traditional "hours" for prayer. The complete cycle may be used when on retreat, at times when special attention to spiritual discipline is important to our growth, or as a reminder that day and night can be permeated with prayer. The historic Great Litany, based on the litany of Thomas Cranmer, is included as well.

Individuals and chapters are encouraged to use these offices as guides and resources. While they have been developed for members of The Order of Saint Luke, they are commended to those outside The Order as well, with the hope that they will help us all to "pray without ceasing."

The editor wishes to express special appreciation to Brother Thomas Rand who served as editorial assistant for the first edition of this volume, to Judy Russell who prepared the manuscript, and to Garrett-Evangelical Theological Seminary for their support of this project. I am also grateful to the contributors listed below, especially Brother Daniel T. Benedict for his prayers, Brother Larry Clinton Seybold (of blessed memory) and Brother Gregory Hayes for their collects, Brother John Fahey for his preparation of a Vigil for the Eve of the Lord's Day, and Brother Timothy Crouch for his adaptations of traditional prayers, as well as his "Thanksgivings and Supplications." The support of this project and the careful work of Brother Timothy and Sister Nancy Crouch in the production process has been, and continues to be, a blessing to the life and work of The Order of Saint Luke.

We share our work with you in the name of the holy and blessed Trinity, with the prayer that the Holy Spirit will guide both our efforts and your use of these resources. "Unless the Lord builds the house, they labor in vain who build it."

Dwight W. Vogel, O.S.L.
Garrett-Evangelical Theological Seminary
2121 Sheridan Road
Evanston, IL 60201
Feast of the Presentation, 2001

Contributors:

E. Byron Anderson, O.S.L.	(EBA)
Daniel T. Benedict, O.S.L.	(DTB)
Barbara Braley, O.S.L.	(BB)
Donald F. Chatfield	(DFC)
Timothy J. Crouch, O.S.L.	(TJC)
Arlo D. Duba	(ADD)
Jennifer Dust Cottrill, O.S.L.	(JDC)
Elmer Lee Eveland, O.S.L.	(ELE)
Allan J. Ferguson	(AJF)
Sarah Flynn, O.S.L.	(SF)
Clifton F. Guthrie, O.S.L.	(CFG)
Gregory L. Hayes, O.S.L.	(GLH)
Schuyler J. Lowe-McCracken, O.S.L.	(SJL)
William P. McDonald, O.S.L.	(WPM)
Brian O'Grady, O.S.L.	(BO)
David N. Power, O.M.L.	(DNP)
Thomas A. Rand, O.S.L.	(TAR)
George E. Reed, O.S.L.	(GER)
Larry Clinton Seybold, O.S.L.	(LCS)
Dwight W. Vogel, O.S.L.	(DWV)
Kimberly Anne Willis, O.S.L.	(KAW)

Guidance for Use in Community

1. Collects and times of prayer may be introduced with the following dialogue:
The Lord be with you.
And also with you.
Let us pray.

2. The Apostles' Creed or another of the statements of the Christian Faith may be used following the Canticle in Morning or Evening Prayer.

3. When the Lord's Prayer is sung, the Blessing and Dismissal may precede the closing hymn. The Lord's Prayer may be transferred to the beginning of the time of prayer; however, it should either begin or end the community's prayer time.

4. The passing of the peace may conclude any office when it seems appropriate.

The Liturgical Psalter

The International Commission on English in the Liturgy has provided a recent translation for psalms and canticles which is particularly sensitive to their use in public prayer and worship. We are delighted to have received permission to use them in this Daily Office. They speak in new ways about depths of human response inherent in the psalms and canticles. Here we discover again why psalms and canticles have been at the heart of daily prayer since the time of the early Church.

In the course of the Daily Office across an entire year, all one hundred fifty psalms are used at least once. While I recognize the value of using the entire psalter, I also have some appreciation of John Wesley's discomfort with the use of some parts of the psalms in Christian worship. I have sought to find a middle road. In the long run, all verses of all psalms will be used. But in particular offices, selections of relevant portions of psalms will sometimes be made. I have endeavored to do this infrequently, however, including some of the "raw edges" which make us pause and reflect on our own responses.

Singing the psalms and canticles:

Persons desiring to use the "psalm tone" form of chanting will find that an underline has replaced the traditional "point" as an indication of where one is to move from the reciting tone, as well as indicating how many syllables are to be sung to the first note after the reciting tone. The syllable or syllables between what is underlined and what is italicized are sung to the second note after the reciting tone. The syllable(s) printed in italics are to be sung to the last note of the cadence or half-cadence. When a "- " appears after a word, the syllable before the hyphen is sung to two notes.

The psalms and canticles may also be sung to "simplified Anglican chant." Ignore the underlined syllable(s), and move to the concluding note of the phrase on the italicized syllable(s). Whenever possible, the text has been arranged in groups which have four italicized portions, thus enabling them to be sung to a four section simplified chant.

[DWV]

Thoughts on the Daily Office rubrics

The Daily Office is constructed (following the ancient pattern of the Western Church) as follows:

Vigil (Matins)
Morning Prayer (Lauds)
Mid-Morning Prayer (Terce)
Mid-Day Prayer (Sext)
Mid-Afternoon Prayer (None)
Evening Prayer (Vespers)
Night Prayer (Compline)

In accordance with Jewish custom, the Church begins and concludes the celebration of Sundays (The Lord's Day) and Solemn Festivals with the evening service or 1st and 2nd Evening Prayer (Vespers), which along with Vigil (Matins) and Morning Prayer (Lauds) are the most ancient and solemn of the canonical hours.

Thus, in the Daily Office the 1st Evening Prayer (Vespers) of Sunday is said on Saturday Evening and the 2nd Evening Prayer (Vespers) is said on Sunday Evening. The Daily Office also offers Sanctoral Solemnities which follow the same pattern

The Daily Office's observances may be classified as follows:

1. SUNDAYS — which are never superceded by a sanctoral festival save for All Saints' Day, which may be celebrated on the First Sunday in November.

2. SOLEMNITIES — have their own proper office; usually a Vigil or Solemn Vespers, Morning Prayer, and a reading found in *For All the Saints* (Volume V in this series) which may be read at Morning or Evening Prayer. Solemnities which fall on a Sunday are transferred to the following Monday or as indicated in the office.

3.   FEASTS — have their own proper scripture readings, psalm and Collects, as well as a reading in *For All The Saints*. On Feasts, the Office of the weekday is said, but one of the proper collects is used in place of the Morning Prayer and Concluding Collect at Morning Prayer, and the Concluding Collect at Evening Prayer. Likewise the Proper scripture lessons for the Feast are used in place of the weekday readings. Feasts do not have a 1st Evening Prayer (Vespers). Feasts which fall on Sundays are transferred (like Solemnities) to the following Monday.

4.   COMMEMORATIONS — have a collect (to be prayed in its suggested place at Morning and Evening Prayer) and a reading from *For All the Saints* to be used at either Office. Commemorations which fall on Sundays are suppressed for that year, and Commemorations which fall on Saturday or the day before a Solemnity are remembered only at Morning Prayer.

On Sundays and Solemnities the Office begins with 1st Evening Prayer (Vespers) on the evening before or with Vigil (which can take the place of 1st Evening Prayer [Vespers] and Night Prayer [Compline]), and it ends with 2nd Evening Prayer on the day itself.

On Weekdays, Feasts, and Commemorations, the Office begins with Morning Prayer of the Day itself and concludes with Evening Prayer.

This is the pattern used in *The Roman Daily Office* as well as *The Book of Common Prayer* and *The Lutheran Book of Worship*.

John P. Fahey, Jr. O.S.L.
taken from Vol. XII, No. 4, of *Sacramental Life*

Ordinary Of The Hours

Together with Seasonal Propers

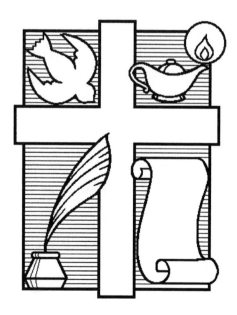

Evening Prayer
(Vespers or Evensong)

ENTRANCE OF THE LIGHT
  Light and peace in Jesus Christ!
  Thanks be to God!
  (See propers for the day)

HYMN OF LIGHT *(The "Phos hilaron;" see front cover)*

[THANKSGIVING FOR LIGHT *(On Saturday and Sunday evenings)*
  Blessed are you, O Lord our God. In every age you have written our history in water. From the chaos of the seas you brought forth our world. From the midst of the Red Sea you gave birth to a people. Through the Jordan you brought Israel to a promised land and sent forth your Son to be the anointed who would proclaim the good news of your kingdom. In these days you again recreate and form us. In the memorial of Christ's death and rising, new sons and daughters prepare to be born from the font, the womb of your church. Thanks be to you through Jesus our crucified and risen Lord in the life-giving love of the Holy Spirit this eventide and for ever and ever. Amen.
  [BY PERMISSION OF ALLELUIA PRESS; ALT.]

[INCENSE
[An angel, holding a golden censer full of incense, stood before the altar. The smoke of the incense went up before God, mingled with the prayers of the people. (Revelation 8:3-4)]

EVENING PRAYER CANTICLE *(selected from Psalm 141)*

A. CHANT FORM: *(see front cover)*
  (See UMH, *bottom of p. 850 for a musical setting of the antiphon by Arlo Duba)*

B: METRICAL FORM: [8888.88; tune: ST. PETERSBURG *UMH* 153]

> Come quickly, Lord, I call on you;
> And hear my voice, my cry for help.
> Control my lips and tongue, O Lord,
> And save my heart from evil's grasp.
> Let my prayer rise like incense, Lord,
> My hands, an ev'ning sacrifice.

Help me accept rebuke as grace,
And guard me from all bitterness.
All wicked ways may I resist
And never share in sensuous feasts.
Let my prayer rise like incense, Lord,
My hands, an ev'ning sacrifice.

Protect me from the Evil One,
And rule my life through Christ your Son,
With Holy Fire my sins consume,
And flood my soul with love divine,
My heart shall rise as incense, Lord,
My life, your living sacrifice.

[SF]

CONFESSION AND PARDON *(See propers for the day)*

INVITATORY AND PSALTER
   O God, come to our assistance.
   O Lord, hasten to help us.
   Glory to you, O Trinity, most holy and blessed;
   One God, now and forever. Amen.

   (See propers of the day for the psalter)

THE GLORIA *(see back cover; musical setting, UMH 72; or:)*
Glory to God, Love abounding be-<u>fore</u> all *ages;*
Glory to God, Love shown forth in the self-emptying of <u>Je</u>-sus *Christ;*
Glory to God, Love poured out through the <u>gift</u> of the *Spirit,*
   who fashions and renews the <u>face</u> of the *earth;*
Glory to the holy and <u>bless</u>-ed *Trinity!*
All things abiding in Love,
   Love abiding <u>in</u> all *things,*
As it is now, <u>ev</u>-er *was,*
   and ever shall be for endless <u>ages.</u> A-*men.*

[DNP]

SCRIPTURE(S) and SILENT REFLECTION

CANTICLE OF MARY (The *Magnificat;* Luke 1:39-56)
   (see UMH 198-200, and Stanza 4 of 197 for metrical versions)

CHANT FORM A: (see front cover)

    I acclaim the greatness <u>of</u> the *Lord,*
    I delight in <u>God</u> my *savior,*
    who regarded my <u>hum</u>-ble *state.*
    Truly from this day on all ages will <u>call</u> me *blest.*

    For God, wonderful in power, has used that <u>strength</u> for *me.*
    Holy the name <u>of</u> the *Lord!*
    whose mercy em-<u>braces</u> the *faithful,*
    one generation <u>to</u> the *next.*

    The mighty arm of God scatters the proud in <u>their</u> con-*ceit,*
    pulls tyrants from their thrones, and raises <u>up</u> the *humble.*
    The Lord <u>fills</u> the *starving*
    and lets the <u>rich</u> go *hungry.*

    God rescues <u>low</u>-ly *Israel,*
    recalling the <u>promise</u> of *mercy,*
    the promise made <u>to</u> our *ancestors,*
    to Abraham's <u>heirs</u> for *ever.*   [ICEL]

    Glory to you, O Trinity, most <u>holy</u> and *blessed:*
        One God, now and for <u>ever.</u> A-*men.*   [TJC]

[READING(S) FOR MEDITATION AND REFLECTION

PRAYERS

[*When prayed in community, the time of prayer begins with this dialogue:*
  The Lord be with you.
    And also with you.
  Let us pray.
    (*See propers for the day*)

—*silent prayer*—

[OTHER SELECTED PRAYERS (*from the following or other resources*)

THE COLLECT FOR PEACE
Most holy God, the source of all good desires, all right judgements, and all just works; Give to us, your servants, that peace which the world cannot give, so that our minds may be fixed on the doing of your will, and the fear of our enemies having been removed, we may pass our time in rest and quietness; Through the mercies of Jesus Christ our Savior. **Amen.**   [GELASIAN SACRAMENTARY, 8TH CENTURY, ALT. TJC]

THE COLLECT FOR AID AGAINST PERILS
O God, the life of all who live, the light of the faithful, the strength of those who labor, and the repose of the dead: We thank you for the

blessings of the day that is past and humbly ask for your protection through the coming night. Bring us in safety to the morning hours; Through him who died and rose again for us, our Savior Jesus Christ. **Amen.**   [Mozarabic Sacramentary, 6th Century]

[PRAYERS OF SPECIAL INTENTION (*such as the following:*)
   [Collect of Commemoration (*see pages 30ff*)
   [Intercessions for the Order of Saint Luke:

   Hear our prayer and let our cry come to you:
   for Brother/Sister _____ our Abbot;
   for the Officers of the General Chapter, _____;
   for Brother/Sister _____ our Prior;
   for our brothers and sisters in the Order
     [especially . . .];
   for a sense of connectedness with others in the Order;
   for grace to live for you and with each other
    in keeping our Rule of Life and Service;
   Lord in your mercy,
    hear our prayer.   [DBT, DWV]

[A Collect for the Order of Saint Luke (*see p. 248*)

Concluding Collect (*See propers for the day*)

The Lord's Prayer
   (*See p. 248; see* UMH *270-271 for musical settings*)

Our Father in heaven,
   hallowed be your name,
   your kingdom come,
   your will be done, on earth as in heaven.
Give us today our daily bread.
Forgive us our sins
   as we forgive those who sin against us.
Save us from the time of trial
   and deliver us from evil.
For the kingdom, the power, and the glory are yours
   now and forever. Amen.

HYMN (*See propers for the day*)

GOING FORTH (*See propers for the day*)
   Let us bless the Lord.
   Thanks be to God!

Compline

(Night Prayer)

CALL TO PRAYER

O God, come to our assistance.
O Lord, hasten to help us.
The Lord almighty grant us a restful night,
and peace at the last.
Amen.

NIGHT HYMN   [87.87; Tune: STUTTGART, *UMH* 611]

Savior, breathe an evening blessing
'Ere repose our spirits seal;
Sin and want we come confessing;
Thou canst save, and thou canst heal.

Though destruction walk around us,
Though the arrows past us fly,
Angel guards from thee surround us;
We are safe, if thou art nigh.

Though the night be dark and dreary,
Darkness cannot hide from thee;
Thou art Christ who, never weary,
Watches where thy people be.

Blessed Spirit, brooding o'er us,
Chase the darkness of our night,
Till the perfect day before us
Breaks in everlasting light.

[J. EDMESTON, 1820]

CONFESSION AND ASSURANCE

O thou, most holy and beloved,
my Companion, my Guide upon the way,
my bright evening star:
We repent the wrongs we have done.

We have wounded your love.
O God, heal us.
We stumble in the darkness.
Light of the world transfigure us.
We forget that we are your home.
Spirit of God, dwell in us.

Eternal Spirit, living God,
in whom we live and move and have our being,
all that we are, have been, and shall be is known to you,
to the very secrets of our hearts
and all that rises to trouble us.
Living flame, burn into us,
cleansing wind, blow through us,
fountain of water, well up within us,
that we may love and praise in deed and in truth.

[ANZPB-HKMOA]

—a time of silence—

We are a forgiven people!
Thanks be to God!

PSALTER (*one or more of the following psalms*)

Our help is in the name of the Lord;
who made heaven and earth.

Psalm 4

Answer when I <u>call</u>, faithful *God.*
You cleared a-<u>way</u> my *trouble;*
be <u>good</u> to *me,*
listen <u>to</u> my *prayer.*

How long, proud fools,
    will you in-<u>sult</u> my *honor,*
loving lies and <u>chas</u>-ing *shadows?*
Look! God a-<u>stounds</u> be-*lievers,*
the Lord listens <u>when</u> I *call.*

Tremble, but do <u>not</u> de-*spair.*
Attend to your heart, be calm <u>through</u> the *night,*
worship <u>with</u> in-*tegrity,*
trust <u>in</u> the *Lord.*

Cynics ask, "Who will bless us?
    Even God has <u>turned</u> a-*way.*"
You give my heart more joy
    than all their <u>grain</u> and *wine.*
I sleep se-<u>cure</u> at *night,*
    you keep me <u>in</u> your *care.*

Psalm 91

All you sheltered <u>by the</u> Most *High,*
who live in Al-<u>mighty</u> God's *shadow,*
say to the Lord, "My <u>refuge</u>, my *fortress,*
my God in <u>whom</u> I *trust!"*

God will free you from <u>hunt</u>-ers' *snares,*
will save you from <u>dead</u>-ly *plague,*
will cover you like a <u>nest</u>-ing *bird.*
God's <u>wings</u> will *shelter you.*

No nighttime terror <u>shall</u> you *fear,*
no arrows <u>shot</u> by *day,*
no plague that <u>prowls</u> the *dark,*
no wasting <u>scourge</u> at *noon.*

A thousand may <u>fall</u> at your *side,*
ten thousand <u>at</u> your *right hand.*
But you shall <u>live</u> un-*harmed:*
God is <u>stur</u>-dy *armor.*

You have only to <u>open</u> your *eyes*
to see how the <u>wicked</u> are re-*paid.*
You have the <u>Lord</u> as *refuge,*
have made the Most <u>High</u> your *stronghold.*

No evil shall <u>e</u>-ver *touch you,*
no harm come <u>near</u> your *home.*
God <u>in</u>-structs *angels*
to guard you where-<u>ever</u> you *go.*

With their <u>hands</u> they su-*pport you,*
so your foot will not <u>strike</u> a *stone.*
You will tread on <u>lion</u> and *viper,*
trample tawny <u>lion</u> and *dragon.*

"I deliver all who cling to me,
  raise the ones who <u>know</u> my *name,*
answer those who call me,
  stand with <u>those</u> in *trouble.*
These I <u>rescue</u> and *honor,*
satisfy with long life,
  and show my <u>power</u> to *save."*

Psalm 134

Bless <u>the</u> - *Lord,*
all who <u>serve in</u> God's *house,*
who <u>stand</u> - *watch*
through-<u>out</u> the *night.*

Lift up your hands
  in the <u>ho</u>-ly *place*
and <u>bless</u> the *Lord.*
And may God,
  the maker of <u>earth</u> and *sky,*
bless <u>you</u> from *Zion.*

THE GLORIA (*see back cover, or:*)
  Glory to the blessed and <u>ho</u>-ly *Trinity:*
  One God now and for-<u>ever.</u> A-*men.*

SCRIPTURE
(A brief passage such as:
  2 Corinthians 4:6-10; Ephesians 3:14-19; or Matthew 6:31-34)

The Word of the Lord.
  Thanks be to God!

—silent reflection—

PRAYERS

THE KYRIE (*See* UMH 482-484 *for musical settings*)
  Kyrie eleison, Kyrie eleison, Kyrie eleison.
  Christe eleison, Christe eleison, Christe eleison.
  Kyrie eleison, Kyrie eleison, Kyrie eleison
                        or:
  Lord, have mercy upon us.
    Christ, have mercy upon us.
  Lord, have mercy upon us.

[A TIME OF SILENT AND/OR FREE PRAYER, *concluding with these prayers:*

PRAYER FOR THE SPIRIT'S PRESENCE
Be present, Spirit of God, within us, your dwelling place and home,
that this house may be one where all darkness is penetrated by your
light, all troubles calmed by your peace, all evil redeemed by your

love, all pain transformed in your suffering, and all dying glorified in your risen life. **Amen.**

[ANZPB-HKMOA]

PRAYER FOR THE NIGHT
Visit this place, O Lord, and deliver us from every snare of the enemy. May your angels be round about us to guard us in peace and let your blessing be upon us always; through Christ our Lord. **Amen.**

[ADAPTED FROM THE ROMAN BREVIARY]

THE LORD'S PRAYER
(*See p. 248; See UMH 270-271 for musical settings*)

HYMN   [84.84.888.4; Tune: AR HYD Y NOS, *UMH* 688]

God that madest earth and heaven, darkness and light,
who the day for toil hast given, for rest the night.
May thine angel guards defend us,
slumber sweet thy mercy send us,
holy dreams and hopes attend us
this live-long night.

When the constant sun returning unseals our eyes,
may we born anew like morning, to labor rise.
Gird us for the task that calls us,
let not ease and self enthrall us,
strong through thee whate'er befall us,
O God most wise!

[REGINALD HEBER, 1783-1826]

COMMENDATION
In peace we will lie down and sleep.
In the Lord alone we safely rest.
Guide us waking, O Lord, and guard us sleeping,
that awake we may watch with Christ,
and asleep we may rest in peace.
May the divine help remain with us always.
And with those who are absent from us.

—silence—

Into your hands, O Lord, I commend my spirit,
For you have redeemed me, O Lord,
O God of Truth.

[SARUM BREVIARY, PS. 4:8 AND 30:5, ADAPTED]

CANTICLE OF SIMEON (*The Nunc Dimittis; Luke 2:29-32*)
  (*See* UMH 225 *for a metrical version*)

Lord, you have now set your <u>ser</u>-vant free
  to go in peace as <u>you</u> have *promised;*
for these eyes of mine have <u>seen</u> the Savior,
  Whom you have prepared for all the <u>world</u> to *see.*
A Light to en-<u>lighten</u> the *nations,*
And the glory of your <u>peo</u>-ple *Israel.*

[ICET]

GOING FORTH
  May Almighty God, the blessed and holy Trinity,
  guard and bless us. Let us bless the Lord.
    Thanks be to God!

Vígíl

The Vigil office may be prayed in several ways:
(1) On Saturday evenings, or on the evening before a feast day, holy day, or
special commemoration, it may replace Evening Prayer and Compline
(2) It may serve as a mid-night office in its own right.
(3) It may serve as the basis for an all night vigil, beginning with Evening
Prayer and ending with Morning Prayer (the office of Compline being su-
perceded).

CALL TO WORSHIP
   (If the Vigil Office replaces Evening Prayer, the following should be replaced
   with the Entrance of the Light, The Hymn of Light and the Evening Prayer
   Canticle [see Cover 2], and the Prayer of the Day. Otherwise the following
   is used:)

O Lord, open my lips,
   and my mouth shall proclaim Your praise.
O God, come to our assistance.
   O Lord, hasten to help us.
Glory to you, O Trinity, most holy and blessed:
   one God, now and forever. Amen.

CANTICLE OF PRAISE TO GOD   [*or a suitable hymn or canticle*]
   (*The* Venite Exultemus; *Psalm 95:1-7; 96:8b, 9, 13b*)
   (*For a four-part musical version, see* UMH 91)

Come, sing with <u>joy</u> to *God,*
shout to our <u>savior,</u> our *rock.*
Enter God's <u>presence</u> with *praise,*
enter with <u>shouting</u> and *song.*

A great God is the Lord, over the <u>gods</u> like a *king.*
God cradles the depths of the earth, holds fast the <u>moun</u>-tain *peaks.*
God shaped the <u>ocean</u> and *owns it,*
formed the <u>earth</u> by *hand.*

Come, bow <u>down</u> and *worship,*
kneel to the <u>Lord</u> our *maker.*
This is our <u>God,</u> our *shepherd,*
we are the flock <u>led</u> with *care.*

Bring gifts to the temple, bow down, <u>all</u> the *earth*,
tremble in God's <u>ho</u>-ly *presence*.
[The Lord] comes to <u>judge</u> the *nations*,
to set the earth aright, restoring the <u>world</u> to *order*.

[ICEL]

THE BLESSING

Lord, grant us your blessing.
Let us pray:
Kindle in our hearts, O God,
the flame of that love which never ceases,
that it may burn in us, giving light to others.
May we shine for ever in your temple,
set on fire with your eternal light,
even your Son Jesus Christ,
our Saviour and our Redeemer. **Amen.** [St. Columba, CCP]

THE LESSONS

[In a long vigil, nine lessons may be read. They may be taken from the psalms, be selected according to the season, or be "lectio continua" (continuing readings taken from one Biblical book). On holy festivals, the readings proclaim salvation history (see propers for the day). Each reading is followed by a time of silence, after which a hymn may be sung.]
[Otherwise, three brief lessons may be read, each followed by a time of silence. During Lent, the Te Deum Laudamus *may be replaced by]*

CANTICLE OF REDEMPTION (*De Profumdis*)

Out of the depths I cry to you, O God;
Lord, <u>hear</u> my *voice*.
Incline your ear to the voice of my <u>sup</u>-pli-*cation*.
If you were to mark all iniquities,
O God, <u>who</u> could *stand?*
But there is forgiveness with you
that you <u>may</u> be *worshiped*.

I wait for the Lord, <u>my</u> soul *waits*,
and in God's <u>word</u> I *hope*;
My soul waits for the Lord
more than those who watch <u>for</u> the *morning*;
more than those who watch <u>for</u> the *morning*.

O Israel, trust <u>in</u> the *Lord*;
with God there is mercy and plen-<u>teous</u> re-*demption*
for <u>the -</u> *Lord*
will redeem Israel from <u>all</u> in-*iquities*.

(Psalm 130; alt DWV)

Versicles and responses traditionally used at the conclusion of the Te Deum continue to be used in Lent:

Save your people, Lord, and bless your inheritance.
Govern and uphold them now and always.
Day by day we bless you.
We praise your name forever.
Keep us today, Lord, from all sin.
Have mercy on us, Lord, have mercy.
Lord, show us your love and mercy;
for we put our trust in you.
In you, Lord, is our hope:
and we shall never hope in vain.

[Here other prayers and collects, or The Great Litany (see pages 25ff) may be used. In an all-night vigil, the remainder of the office is superceded by Morning Prayer.]

THE LORD'S PRAYER
(See p. 248; see UMH 270-271 for musical settings)

[NIGHT PRAYERS
When the office of Compline is not prayed, the Commendation Prayer and the Canticle of Simeon (see page 11) are included here.

CONCLUDING PRAYERS
O Lord, hear my prayer,
And let my cry come to you.
Listen to the prayers of your servants;
have mercy on us, Lord Jesus Christ.
Let us bless the Lord.
Thanks be to God!
May the souls of the faithful departed,
through the mercy of God, rest in peace.
Amen.

Morning Prayer
(Lauds)

CALL TO PRAISE AND PRAYER
O Lord, open my lips,
And my mouth shall proclaim your praise.

(See propers of the day)

HYMN *(See propers of the day)*

MORNING PRAYER *(See propers of the day)*

INVITATORY AND PSALTER
O God, come to our assistance.
O Lord, hasten to help us.
Glory to you, O Trinity, most holy and blessed;
One God, now and forever. Amen.
(See propers of the day for the psalter)

THE GLORIA *(see cover 3; musical setting, UMH 72; or:)*
Glory to God, Love abounding be-<u>fore</u> all *ages;*
Glory to God, Love shown forth in the self-emptying of <u>Je</u>-sus *Christ;*
Glory to God, Love poured out through the <u>gift</u> of the *Spirit,*
   who fashions and renews the <u>face</u> of the *earth;*
Glory to the holy and <u>bless</u>-ed *Trinity!*
All things abiding in Love,
   Love abiding <u>in</u> all *things,*
As it is now, <u>ev</u>-er *was,*
   and ever shall be for endless ages. <u>A</u>-*men.*

[DNP]

SCRIPTURE READING(S) AND SILENT REFLECTION

CANTICLE OF ZECHARIAH (The *Benedictus*)
(See UMH 208/209 for metrical versions)

CHANT FORM A: *(see back cover)*

CHANT FORM B:
Praise the Lord, the <u>God</u> of *Israel,*
who shepherds the people and <u>sets</u> them *free.*
God raises from <u>Da</u>-vid's *house*
a child with <u>power</u> to *save.*

Through the ho-ly *prophets*
God promised in a-ges *past*
to save us from ene-my *hands,*
from the grip of all who *hate us.*

The Lord favored our ancestors
   recalling the sa-cred *covenant,*
the pledge to our ancestor Abraham,
   to free us from our *enemies,*
so we might worship without *fear*
and be holy and just all our *days.*

And you, child, will be called
   Prophet of the Most - *High,*
for you will come to prepare
   a pathway for the *Lord*
by teaching the people sal-*vation*
through forgiveness of their *sin.*

Out of God's deepest *mercy*
a dawn will come from on *high,*
light for those shadowed by *death,*
a guide for our feet on the way to *peace.*

[ICEL]

Glory to you, O Trinity, most holy and *blessed:*
   One God, now and for ever. A-*men.*

[TJC]

[READING(S) FOR MEDITATION AND REFLECTION

PRAYERS
[When prayed in community, the time of prayer begins with this dialogue:
   The Lord be with you.
   And also with you.
   Let us pray.
   (See propers for the day)

   SILENT PRAYER

   [OTHER SELECTED PRAYERS

THE COLLECT FOR PEACE
Almighty God,
from whom all thoughts of truth and peace do come:
Pour into the hearts of all people, we pray,
the true love of peace;
and guide with your wisdom
those who take counsel for the nations of the earth,
that in tranquility your work may go forward
until the world is filled with the knowledge of your love;
Through Jesus Christ our Lord. **Amen.**

[BISHOP FRANCIS PAGET, 1851-1911, ALT TJC]

THE COLLECT FOR GRACE
O God, by whom we are guided in judgement,
and who raises up for us light in the darkness:
Grant us, in all our doubts and uncertainties,
the grace to ask what you would have us to do;
that your Spirit of Wisdom may save us from all false choices,
and in your straight path we may not stumble;
Through Jesus Christ our Lord. **Amen.**

[JOHN W. SUTER, JR., INSPIRED BY IS. 30:15 AND PS. 46:11;
FROM SERVICES FOR TRIAL USE: SERIES THREE, 1973,
OF THE CHURCH OF ENGLAND; ALT TJC]

[PRAYERS OF SPECIAL INTENTION *(such as the following:)*
  [COLLECT OF COMMEMORATION *(see pages 30ff)*
  [INTERCESSIONS FOR THE ORDER OF SAINT LUKE *(see back cover)*
  [A COLLECT FOR THE ORDER OF SAINT LUKE *(see p. 248)*

CONCLUDING COLLECT   *(See propers for the day)*

THE LORD'S PRAYER
(See p. 248; see UMH *270-271 for musical settings)*

HYMN *(See propers for the day)*

DISMISSAL AND BLESSING OR ASCRIPTION OF PRAISE
  (See propers for the day)
    Let us bless the Lord.
      Thanks be to God!

Mid-Morning Prayer

(Terce)

OPENING SENTENCES

O God, come to our assistance.
O Lord, hasten to help us.
Glory to the blessed and holy Trinity;
One God now and forever. Amen.

PRAYER

Holy Spirit,
Come upon us this hour without delay;
Pour out your graces on our souls.
Let tongue and soul and mind and strength proclaim your praise.
Set our love aflame by the fire of your love,
and may its warmth enkindle love in our neighbors.
Empower us with your presence
in the name of Christ. **Amen.**

[FROM THE HYMN FOR THIS HOUR ATTRIBUTED
TO ST. AMBROSE, 340-397, ADAPTED BY DWV]

PSALTER Psalm 117

Praise! Give <u>glory</u> to *God!*
Nations, <u>peoples</u>, give *glory!*

Strong the <u>love</u> em-*bracing us.*
Faithful the Lord for ever.
   <u>Hal</u>-le-*lujah!*

THE "LITTLE CHAPTER" A Canticle from Ezekiel 36:24-28

I will draw you from the nations,
gather you from exile
and bring you home.

I will wash you in fresh water,
rid you from the filth of idols
and make you clean again.

I will make you a new heart,
breathe new spirit into you.
I will remove your heart of stone,
give you back a heart of flesh.

I will give you my own spirit
to lead you in my ways,
faithful to what I command.

Then you will live in the land,
the land I gave your ancestors.
You will be my people
and I will be your God.

[ICEL]

—*A Brief Time of Silence*—

[FREE PRAYER]

[THE LORD'S PRAYER
  (See p. 248; see UMH *270-271 for musical settings)*

CONCLUDING PRAYER:
  Living God, in whom we live and move and have our being:
  Guide and govern us by your Holy Spirit,
  so that in all the cares and occupations of our life
  we may not forget you,
  but remember that we are ever walking in your sight;
  through Jesus Christ our Lord. **Amen.**

[BCP, ALT BY DWV]

Let us bless the Lord!
  Thanks be to God!

Mid-Day Prayer
(Sext)

OPENING SENTENCES

O God, come to our assistance.
O Lord, hasten to help us.
Glory to the blessed and holy Trinity;
One God now and forever. Amen.

ACT OF PRAISE

Praise the Lord! Praise, O servants <u>of</u> the *Lord*,
Praise the name <u>of</u> the *Lord!*

Blessed be the name <u>of</u> the Lord
from this time forth and for <u>ev</u>-er-*more*.
From the rising of the sun <u>to</u> its setting
the name of the Lord is <u>to</u> be *praised!*

(Psalm 113:1-4)

COLLECT

Living and dying, Lord, we would be yours;
Keep us as yours for ever,
    and draw us day by day nearer to yourself
    until we are wholly filled with your love
    and fitted to behold you face to face.
Amen.

[ADAPTED FROM A PRAYER BY EDWARD BOUVERIE PUSEY; DTB]

THE *KYRIE* (*See* UMH 482-484 *for musical settings*)

Kyrie eleison, Kyrie eleison, Kyrie eleison.
Christe eleison, Christe eleison, Christe eleison.
Kyrie eleison, Kyrie eleison, Kyrie eleison.

or

Lord, have mercy upon us.
Christ, have mercy upon us.
Lord, have mercy upon us.

[SCRIPTURE(S) *(Selected)*] *and/or*
  THE "LITTLE CHAPTER:"
  Even those who are young grow weak;
    the young can fall exhausted.
  But those who wait on the Lord for help
  will find their strength renewed.
    They will rise on wings like eagles;
  they will run and not get weary;
    they will walk and not grow weak.

(Isaiah 40:30-31)

—A Brief Time of Silence—

[FREE PRAYER]

THE LORD'S PRAYER
  (See p. 248; see UMH 270, 271 for musical settings)

[HYMN

CONCLUDING PRAYER:
  Send forth your Spirit, Lord,
    Renew the face of the earth.
  Creator Spirit, come,
    Inflame our waiting hearts.
  Lord, hear our prayer.
    And let our cry come to You.
  Bless the Lord.
    Thanks be to God!

Mid-Afternoon Prayer

(None)

OPENING SENTENCES
  O God, come to our assistance.
  O Lord, hasten to help us.
  Glory to the blessed and holy Trinity;
  One God now and forever. Amen.

PRAYER
  Living, loving God:
  Through your wisdom the hours of the day move on,
  and there is yet much to do.
  Keep us in your care and renew us with your strength
  so that we may not forget you
  nor be unaware of your love towards those around us.
  In the name of Christ who lives and reigns
  with you and the Holy Spirit.   **Amen.**   [DWV]

[PSALTER: Psalm 1
  If you would be happy: never <u>walk</u> with the *wicked,*
  never stand with sinners, never <u>sit a-</u>mong *cynics,*
  but delight <u>in the</u> Lord's *teaching*
  and study it <u>night</u> and *day.*

  You will stand like a tree <u>planted</u> by a *stream,*
  bearing <u>fruit</u> in *season,*
  its <u>leaves</u> never *fading,*
  its yield <u>al</u>-ways *plenty.*

  Not so for the wicked, like chaff they are <u>blown</u> by the *wind.*
  They will not withstand the judgment,
    nor assemble <u>with</u> the *just.*
  The Lord marks the <u>way</u> of the *upright,*
  but the corrupt <u>walk</u> to *ruin.*

THE "LITTLE CHAPTER:"   A Canticle from Philippians 2:6-11

  Though in the form of God,
  Jesus did not claim
  equality with God
  but emptied himself,
  taking the form of a slave,
  human like one of us.

Flesh and blood,
he humbled himself,
obeying to the death,
death on a cross.

For this very reason
God lifted him high
and gave him the name
above all names.

So at the name of Jesus
every knee will bend
in heaven, on earth,
and in the world below,
and every tongue exclaim
to the glory of God the Father,
"Jesus Christ is Lord."

[ICEL]

—A Brief Time of Silence—

[FREE PRAYER]

[THE LORD'S PRAYER
  (*see p. 248; see* UMH *270, 271 for musical settings*)

CONCLUDING PRAYER:
  Lord Jesus Christ,
  who came to set us free:
  Let the shadow of your cross fall upon us in this hour
  that we may wonder at the gift of your redeeming love,
  rejoice in your resurrection,
  and be empowered by your Spirit
  to take up our own cross daily
  and follow you. **Amen.**

[DWV]

Show us, O God, your mercy,
  And grant us your salvation.
Bless the Lord!
  Thanks be to God!

The Great Litany

Sections I and V are always used; appropriate suffrages may be selected from sections II, III, and IV. The Great Litany in its entirety may replace Mid-day Prayer or Compline, especially if a service of Word and Table is being held close in time. The Great Litany may also be prayed in procession, and may replace the prayers of supplication at any office on Wednesdays or Fridays.

I

O God, creator of heaven and earth,
have mercy upon us.
O God, redeemer of the world,
have mercy upon us.
O God, sanctifier of the faithful,
have mercy upon us.
O holy, blessed, and glorious Trinity, one God,
have mercy upon us.

II

Remember not, Lord Christ, our offenses,
nor the offenses of our forbearers;
do not reward us according to our sins.
Spare us, good Lord, spare your people
whom you have redeemed with your most precious blood;
by your mercy preserve us forever.
  Spare us, good Lord.

From all evil and wickedness;
from sin;
from the crafts and assaults of the devil;
and from everlasting damnation,
  Good Lord, deliver us.

From all blindness of heart;
from pride, vainglory, and hypocrisy;
from envy, hatred, and malice;
and from all want of charity,
  Good Lord, deliver us.

From all inordinate and sinful affections;
and from all the deceits of the world, the flesh, and the devil,
  Good Lord, deliver us.

From all false doctrine, heresy, and schism;
from hardness of heart, and contempt of your Word
and commandment,
   Good Lord, deliver us.

From lightning and tempest; from earthquake, fire, and flood;
from plague, pestilence, and famine,
   Good Lord, deliver us.
From all oppression, violence, battle, and murder;
and from dying suddenly and unprepared,
   Good Lord, deliver us.

By the mystery of your holy incarnation, by your holy nativity;
by your baptism, fasting, and temptation,
   Good Lord, deliver us.

By your agony and bloody sweat;
by your cross and passion;
by your precious death and burial;
by your glorious resurrection and ascension;
and by the coming of your Holy Spirit,
   Good Lord, deliver us.

In all time of our tribulation;
in all time of our prosperity;
in the hour of death, and in the day of judgment,
   Good Lord, deliver us.

III

We beseech you to hear us, Lord God,
that your holy church universal might be governed by you
in the right way.
   We beseech you to hear us, good Lord.

Illumine all bishops, priests and pastors, deacons and ministers,
with true knowledge and understanding of your Word;
that both by their speaking and their living,
they may set it forth, and show it accordingly.
   We beseech you to hear us, good Lord.

Bless and keep all your people.
   We beseech you to hear us, good Lord.

Send forth laborers into your harvest,
and draw all people into your sovereign realm.
   We beseech you to hear us, good Lord.

Give to all people increase of grace
to hear and receive your Word,
and to bring forth the fruits of the Spirit.
We beseech you to hear us, good Lord.

Bring into the way of truth all those who have erred
and are deceived.
We beseech you to hear us, good Lord.

Give us a heart to love and fear you,
and to diligently live according to your commandments.
We beseech you to hear us, good Lord.

Rule the hearts of all those in authority
that they may do justice and love mercy
and walk in the ways of truth.
We beseech you to hear us, good Lord.

Make wars cease in all the world;
give to all nations unity, peace and concord;
and bestow freedom upon all peoples.
We beseech you to hear us, good Lord.

Show pity upon all prisoners and captives,
the homeless and the hungry,
and all who are desolate and oppressed.
We beseech you to hear us, good Lord.

IV

Preserve the bountiful fruits of the earth,
so that all may enjoy them.
We beseech you to hear us, good Lord.

Inspire us, in our several callings,
to do the work you give us to do
with singleness of heart as your servants,
and for the common good.
We beseech you to hear us, good Lord.

Preserve all who are in danger
by reason of their labor or their travel.
We beseech you to hear us, good Lord.

Preserve and provide for all women in childbirth,
young children and orphans, the widows and widowers,
and all whose homes are broken or torn by strife.
We beseech you to hear us, good Lord.

Visit the lonely;
strengthen all who suffer in mind, body and spirit;
and comfort with your presence those who are failing and infirm.
We beseech you to hear us, good Lord.

Support, help, and comfort all who are in danger, and tribulation.
We beseech you to hear us, good Lord.

Have mercy upon all people.
We beseech you to hear us, good Lord.

Give us true repentance;
forgive us all our sins, negligence, and ignorance;
and endue us with the grace of your Holy Spirit
to amend our lives according to your holy Word.
We beseech you to hear us, good Lord.

Forgive our enemies, persecutors, and slanderers,
and turn their hearts.
We beseech you to hear us, good Lord.

Strengthen those who stand;
comfort and help the weak-hearted;
raise up those who fall;
and finally beat down Satan under our feet.
We beseech you to hear us, good Lord.

Grant to all the faithful departed eternal life and peace.
We beseech you to hear us, good Lord.

Grant that in the fellowship of [_____ and]
all the saints, we may enter your heavenly realm.
We beseech you to hear us, good Lord.

V

O Lamb of God, who takes away the sins of the world.
have mercy upon us.
O Lamb of God, who takes away the sins of the world.
have mercy upon us.
O Lamb of God who takes away the sins of the world.
grant us your peace.

[ADAPTED FROM THE 1544 LITANY OF THOMAS CRANMER
WHICH WAS BASED ON THE SARUM ROGATIONTIDE LITANY,
LUTHER'S LATIN LITANY OF 1529,
AND THE DEACON'S LITANY IN THE LITURGY OF ST. JOHN CHRYSOSTOM; BY DWV]

Propers for
Special Feasts
and Observances

For services on Ash Wednesday, see pages 62 *ff*.

For services from Holy Thursday evening through Easter evening,
see Propers for the Tridum, pages 189 *ff*.

NOTE:
Resources for additional commemorations may be found in *For All the Saints*,
which is Volume V of this series.

Compline
(for Lent)

CALL TO PRAYER
  O God, come to our assistance.
  O Lord, hasten to help us.
  The Lord almighty grant us a restful night,
  and peace at the last.
  Amen.

NIGHT HYMN [LM; Tune: CONDITOR ALME SIDERUM, *UMH* 692]

Before the ending of the day,
Creator of the world, we pray:
pour out on all who seek thy face
abundance of thy pardoning grace.

Our hearts are open, Lord, to Thee;
Thou knowest our infirmity.
Give us the self-control that springs
from discipline of outward things.

We pray thee, Holy Trinity,
One God, unchanging Unity:
before thy throne of mercy spent
in this thy holy fast of Lent.

[COMPOSITE: 7TH CENTURY AMBROSIAN, TE LUCIS ANTE TERMINUM (TR. JOHN MASON NEALE);
6TH CENTURY GREGORIAN, AUDI BENIGNE CONDITOR (TR. T.A. LACEY)]

CONFESSION AND ASSURANCE
  O thou, most holy and beloved,
  my Companion, my Guide upon the way,
  my bright evening star:
  We repent the wrongs we have done.

  We have wounded your love.
  O God, heal us.
  We stumble in the darkness.
  Light of the world transfigure us.
  We forget that we are your home.
  Spirit of God, dwell in us.

Eternal Spirit, living God,
in whom we live and move and have our being,
all that we are, have been and shall be is known to you,
to the very secrets of our hearts
and all that rises to trouble us.
Living flame, burn into us,
cleansing wind, blow through us,
fountain of water, well up within us,
that we may love and praise in deed and in truth.

[ANZPB-HKMOA]

-a time of silence-

We are a forgiven people!
Thanks be to God!

PSALTER (*one or more of the following psalms*)
Our help is in the name of the Lord;
who made heaven and earth.

Psalm 4

Answer when I <u>call</u>, faithful *God.*
You cleared a-<u>way</u> my *trouble;*
be <u>good</u> to *me,*
listen <u>to</u> my *prayer.*

How long, proud fools,
   will you in-<u>sult</u> my *honor,*
loving lies and <u>chas</u>-ing *shadows?*
Look! God a-<u>stounds</u> be-*lievers,*
the Lord listens <u>when</u> I *call.*

Tremble, but do <u>not</u> de-*spair.*
Attend to your heart, be calm <u>through</u> the *night,*
worship <u>with</u> in-*tegrity,*
trust <u>in</u> the *Lord.*

Cynics ask, "Who will bless us?
   Even God has <u>turned</u> a-*way."*
You give my heart more joy
   than all their <u>grain</u> and wine.
I sleep se-<u>cure</u> at night,
you keep me <u>in</u> your care.

Psalm 131

Lord, I am not proud,
   holding my <u>head</u> too *high,*
reaching be - <u>yond</u> my *grasp.*
No, I am calm and tranquil
   like a weaned child
   resting in its <u>moth</u> - er's *arms:*
my whole <u>being</u> at *rest.*

Let Israel rest <u>in</u> the *Lord,*
now <u>and</u> for *ever.*

THE GLORIA (*see cover 3; musical setting,* UMH 72; *or:*)
  Glory to the blessed and <u>ho</u>-ly *Trinity:*
  One God now and for-<u>ev</u>er. A-*men.*

SCRIPTURE
(A brief passage such as: Isaiah 55: 6-7; John 6: 66-69; or 1 Peter 2:1-5)

—silent reflection—

PRAYERS

The *Kyrie* (See *UMH* 482-484 for musical settings)

   Kyrie eleison, Kyrie eleison, Kyrie eleison.
   Christe eleison, Christe eleison, Christe eleison.
   Kyrie eleison, Kyrie eleison, Kyrie eleison.

or

Lord, have mercy upon us.
  Christ, have mercy upon us.
Lord, have mercy upon us.

[A Time of Silent and/or Free Prayer, *concluding with these prayers:*

COLLECT
 O Lord, support us all the day long, until the shadows lengthen and
the evening comes, and the busy world is hushed, and the fever of
life is over, and our work is done. Then in your mercy grant us a safe
lodging, and a holy rest, and peace at the last. **Amen.**

                                 [JOHN HENRY NEWMAN, 1801-90]

PRAYER FOR THE NIGHT
Visit this place, O Lord, and deliver us
from every snare of the enemy.
May your angels be round about us to guard us in peace
and let your blessing be upon us always;
through Christ our Lord. **Amen.**

[ADAPTED FROM THE ROMAN BREVIARY]

THE LORD'S PRAYER (*See p. 248*)
   (*See* UMH 270-271 *for musical settings*)

HYMN [84.84.888.4; Tune: AR HYD Y NOS, *UMH* 688]
God that madest earth and heaven, darkness and light,
who the day for toil hast given, for rest the night.
May thine angel guards defend us,
slumber sweet thy mercy send us,
holy dreams and hopes attend us
this live-long night.

When the constant sun returning unseals our eyes,
may we born anew like morning, to labor rise.
Gird us for the task that calls us,
let not ease and self enthrall us,
strong through thee whate'er befall us,
O God most wise!

[REGINALD HEBER, 1783-1826]

COMMENDATION
In peace we will lie down and sleep.
In the Lord alone we safely rest.
Guide us waking, O Lord, and guard us sleeping,
that awake we may watch with Christ,
and asleep we may rest in peace.
May the divine help remain with us always.
And with those who are absent from us.

—silence—

Into your hands, O Lord, I commend my spirit,
For you have redeemed me, O Lord,
O God of Truth.

[SARUM BREVIARY, PSALM 4:8 AND 30:5, ADAPTED]

CANTICLE OF SIMEON (The *Nunc dimittis* Luke 2:29-32)
  (*See* UMH 226 *for a metrical version*)

Lord, you have now set your <u>ser</u>-vant free
  to go in peace as <u>you</u> have *promised;*
for these eyes of mine have <u>seen</u> the Savior,
Whom you have prepared for all the <u>world</u> to see.
A Light to en-<u>lighten</u> the *nations,*
And the glory of your <u>peo</u>-ple *Israel.*

[ICET]

GOING FORTH
  May Almighty God, the blessed and holy Trinity,
  guard and bless us. Let us bless the Lord.
  Thanks be to God!

An Office of Readings

(to be spoken or read silently)

PROLOGUE

We know that the whole creation has been groaning in labor pains until now; and not only the creation, but we ourselves, who have the first fruits of the Spirit, groan inwardly while we wait for adoption, the redemption of our bodies. For in hope we were saved. Now hope that is seen is not hope. For who hopes for what is seen? But if we hope for what we do not see, we wait for it with patience. Likewise the Spirit helps us in our weakness; for we do not know how to pray as we ought, but that very Spirit intercedes with sighs too deep for words. And God, who searches the heart, knows what is the mind of the Spirit, because the Spirit intercedes for the saints according to the will of God.

(Romans 8:22-27)

INVITATION

The Psalms speak to us and for us through praise and lament, thanksgiving and supplication. Yet we find other voices there, too, voices which are hard to hear as prayer to God. In them we find the sinful side of ourselves, of the Church, and of human history. Let us seek for honesty before God, praying for forgiveness for ourselves, for our ancestors in the faith, and for the Church.

CALL TO CONFESSION

> Let us return to the Lord
> who tore us apart
> but now will heal us;
> who struck us down
> yet binds our wounds;
> who revives us after two days,
> raising us up on the third,
> to live in God's presence.
>
> Let us seek to know the Lord,
> whose coming is sure as dawn,
> who descends like the rain,
> spring rain renewing the earth.
>
> What can I do with you, Ephraim?
> What can I do with you Judah?
> Your love is but a morning mist,
> a dew that vanishes early.

So I cut them down by my prophets,
slew them with my words;
my judgment blazes like the sun.
For I take delight
not in sacrifices,
but in loyal love;
not in holocausts,
but in the knowledge of God.

(Hosea 6:1-6 ICEL)

Psalm 39

I

I said I will not sin!
I will curb my tongue
   and muzzle my mouth
   when the wicked confront me.

I kept silent,
   would not say a word,
   yet my anguish grew.
It scorched my heart
   and seared my thoughts
   until I had to speak.

II

Lord, what will become of me?
How long will I live?
Let me see how short life is!

You give me a brief span of time;
   before you, my days are nothing.
People are but a breath:
   they walk like shadows;
   their efforts amount to nothing;
   they hoard, but others gain.

III

Why do I wait for you, Lord?
You are my hope
   to save me from my sins;
   do not make a fool of me.
I will keep quiet.
I have said enough,
   since all this is your doing.

Stop tormenting me;
  you strike and I grow weak.
You rebuke us for our sin,
  eat up our riches like a moth;
  we are but a breath.

Lord, hear my prayer,
  my cry for help.
Do not ignore my tears,
  as if I were alien to you,
  a stranger like my ancestors.
Stop looking so hard at me,
  allow me a little joy
  before I am no more.

—silence—

PSALM PRAYER

God of judgment and of grace: our good intentions are too often overwhelmed by our anguished passions. In our confusion, we do not
separate your word of judgment from the torment we bring on ourselves. Touch us with your healing presence so that both our tears
and our longing for joy may be channels of your grace. In the name
of Christ who came to make us whole, we pray. **Amen.**

Psalm 55

I

Listen, God, to my plea,
  do not ignore my cry.
Listen and answer,
I shake with grief
  at the furor of my enemies.
They threaten and attack me;
  they shout out curses,
  venting their anger against me.

My heart is pounding,
  I can feel the touch of death.
Terror holds me in its grip,
  trembling seizes me.

"If I had wings like a dove,
  I would fly far and rest,
  fly far away to the wilds
  to escape the raging storm."

Confuse their speech, Lord!
I see violence and strife
  stalk their city walls
  both day and night.

Evil and destruction
  live in their midst;
  oppression and deceit
  never leave the public square.

If my enemy insults me,
  I can bear it;
  if a foe rises against me,
  I can hide myself.

But it was you, my own friend,
  the one I knew so well.
With you I could always talk,
  even as we walked to the temple,
  my companion amid the crowd.

II

Death to them all!
Let them fall into Sheol alive,
  for evil fills their homes
  and lives among them.

I call out to God
  who rescues me.
Morning, noon, and night
  I plead my case.

God hears my cry,
  brings me to safety
  when the battle is raging
  and my foes are many.

Enthroned for ever,
  God acts by humbling them
  because they refuse to change;
  they will not fear God.

My friend turned traitor
  and broke old promises,
  spoke words smooth as butter

while intending war,
words that flowed like oil
but cut like a sword.

Give your burden to the Lord,
  who will be your support.
If you are faithful,
  God will not let you fall.

III

O God, hurl the bloodthirsty
  into the pit of destruction.
Let traitors live only half their days.
But as for me, I trust in you.

—silence—

PSALM PRAYER

Lord Jesus Christ, who knew the pain of betrayal and denial from your closest companions: walk with us when friends hurt us. When our anger seeks retribution, tame our troubled spirits so that we are not consumed by our pain, but respond, by your grace, with constructive courage, in your name. **Amen.**

Psalm 69

I

Save me, God!
Water is up to my neck.
I am sinking in mud,
  without a rock to stand on,
  plunged in the deep
  beneath the current.

I am tired of shouting,
  my throat is raw,
  my eyes swollen;
I am worn out waiting for God.

Many hate me without cause,
  they outnumber the hairs on my head.
I have fewer bones
  than I have lying enemies
  who demand I return
  what I did not steal.

II

God, you know my folly,
  my sins are plain to you.

Lord, commander of heaven's army,
  may those who hope in you
  not be shamed because of me.
May those seeking you
  not be humbled on my account,
  Lord God of Israel.

I bear shame and insult
  because I bear your name.
Rejected by my family,
  I am a stranger to my kin.

My passion for your cause
  takes all my strength.
Insults meant for you
  now fall on me.

Despite my tears and fasting,
  I only gained contempt.
My sackcloth made me a joke.
I was the butt of gossips,
  the victim of drunkard's taunts.

III

Lord, hear this prayer,
  favor me now with love,
  and send me your ready help.
Lift me from the mud,
  keep me from sinking,
  let me escape my tormentors
  and rise above the waters.

Do not let the waters drown me,
  the deep swallow me,
  the pit close me in its mouth.
Answer me, Lord,
  turn to me with mercy and love.

Face me, I am desperate.
Answer your servant now,
  come to my rescue,
  free me from my enemies.

You know my disgrace,
   my embarrassment and shame,
   you see my oppressors.

Their insults break my spirit,
   I am sick at heart.
I looked for comfort and sympathy
   but found none.
They poisoned my food,
   and gave me vinegar to drink.

                              IV

Make their table their trap,
   a snare for their friends.
Blind them,
   cripple them,
   rage at them.
Let your anger consume them.
Let their tents be deserted,
   their campsites a graveyard.

For they torment the sick
   and ridicule their pain.
Keep a full record of their guilt;
   none of your mercy for them!
Erase them from the book of life,
   lest they be tallied among the just.

                              V

But I am ill, in pain.
Rescue me, God,
   lift me up.

Then I shall give thanks
   and praise God's name,
   for song pleases God more than cattle
   or bulls with horns and hooves.

Look and see, you oppressed,
   there is cause to rejoice
   for those who seek God.
Let your hearts hope again,
   for the Lord hears the poor,
   does not despise the imprisoned.

Praise God, heaven and earth,
  the seas and all that live in them,
  for God rescues Zion,
  rebuilds the towns of Judah
  for people to own and inhabit.

Their offspring will inherit Judah,
  and those who serve God's name
  will make it their home.

—silence—

PSALM PRAYER
  O God who calls us to faithful service: the cost of discipleship sometimes seems more than we can bear and we lash out at those we think
  are your enemies. Trouble us if our faithfulness never discomforts
  us, but preserve us from feeling martyred at every turn. Help us to
  know that nothing can separate us from your love for us in Jesus Christ,
  in whose name we pray. **Amen.**

Psalm 76
  God, you are known throughout Judah,
  Israel glories in your name.
  Your tent is pitched in Salem,
    your command post on Zion.
  There you break flaming arrows,
    shield and sword and war itself!

  Majestic and circled with light,
    you seize your prey;
  stouthearted soldiers
    are stripped of their plunder.
  Dazed, they cannot lift a hand.
  At your battle cry, God of Jacob,
    horse and rider are stunned.

  You, the one who strikes fear
    who can stand up to your anger!
  Your verdict sounds from heaven;
    earth reels, then is still,
  when you stand as judge
    to defend the oppressed.
  When you are robed in fury,
    even the warlike give you praise.

Now, all you worshippers,
  keep your promise to God,
  bring gifts to the Holy One
  who terrifies princes
  and stuns the rulers of earth.

—silence—

PSALM PRAYER

Awesome God, who destroys war and defends the defenseless: when victory seems to be in the hands only of the oppressors, show us how to stand with you on the side of justice and peace. **Amen.**

Psalm 87

Zion is set on the holy mountain.
The Lord loves her gates
  above all the dwellings of Israel.
Great is your renown, city of God.

I register as her citizens
Egypt and Babylon,
Philistia, Ethiopia, and Tyre:
"Each one was born in her."

People will say, "Zion mothered
  each and every one."
The Most High protects the city.

God records in the register,
  "This one was born here."
Then people will dance and sing,
  "My home is here!"

—silence—

PSALM PRAYER

Let our home be with your people, Covenant God, because you dwell with us. Let the birthright of our baptism mark us as members of your family. In the name of Jesus Christ our brother we pray. **Amen.**

Psalm 135

I

Praise the name of the Lord,
  give praise, faithful servants,
  who stand in the courtyard,
  gathered at God's house.

Sing hymns, for God is good.
Sing God's name, our delight,
   for the Lord chose Jacob,
   Israel as a special treasure.

I know the Lord is great,
   surpassing every little God.
What God wills, God does
   in heaven and earth,
   in the deepest sea.

God blankets earth with clouds,
   strikes lightning for the rain,
   releases wind from the storehouse.

God killed Egypt's firstborn,
   both humans and beasts,
   doing wondrous signs in Egypt
   against Pharoah and his aides.

God struck down nations,
   killed mighty kings,
   Sihon, king of the Amorites,
   Og, king of Bashan,
   all the kings of Canaan.

Then God gave Israel their land,
   a gift for them to keep.
Your name lives for ever, Lord,
   your renown never fades,
   for you give your people justice
   and attend to their needs.

II

Pagan idols are silver and gold
   crafted by human hands.
Their mouths cannot speak,
   their eyes do not see.

Their ears hear nothing,
   their nostrils do not breathe.
Their makers who rely on them
   become like these hollow images.

Bless God, house of Israel,
  house of Aaron, house of Levi,
  every faithful one.

Blest be the Lord of Zion,
  who calls Jerusalem home.

Hallelujah!

—silence—

PSALM PRAYER

We praise your greatness, God of power and might, and give thanks for your liberating acts. We know that liberation must cost the oppressors, but the God made known to us in Jesus Christ does not inflict needless suffering, even on your "enemies." Keep us from making our image of you into another idol, crafted by human minds. Instead, conform us by your saving love to the new creation you would have us be. In Christ's name, we dare to be honest before you. **Amen.**

Psalm 31

I

Shelter me, Lord,
  save me from shame.
Let there be justice:
  save me!

Help me! Listen!
Be quick to the rescue!
Be my fortress, my refuge.

You, my rock and fortress,
  prove your good name.
Guide me, lead me,
  free me from their trap.

You are my shelter;
  I put myself in your hands,
  knowing you will save me,
  Lord God of truth.

You hate the slaves of idols,
  but I trust in you.
I dance for joy at your constant love.

You saw me suffer,
  you know my pain.
You let no enemy cage me,
  but set my feet on open ground.

II

Pity me, Lord,
  I hurt all over;
  my eyes are swollen,
  my heart and body ache.

Grief consumes my life,
  sighs fill my days;
  guilt saps my strength,
  my bones dissolve.

Enemies mock me,
  make me the butt of jokes.
Neighbors scorn me,
  strangers avoid me.
Forgotten like the dead,
  I am a shattered jar.

I hear the crowd whisper,
  "Attack on every side!"
  as they scheme to take my life.

But I trust in you, Lord.
I say, "You are my God,
  my life is in your hands."
Snatch me from the enemy,
  ruthless in their chase.

Look on me with love,
  save your servant.
I call on you;
  save me from shame!

Shame the guilty,
  silence them with the grave.
Silence the lips that lie,
  that scorn the just.

How rich your goodness
  to those who revere you!
The whole world can see:
  whoever seeks your help
  finds how lavish you are.

You are shelter from gossips,
  a place to hide from busy tongues.
Blessed be the Lord!
God's love encircles me
  like a protecting wall.

I said too quickly,
  "God has cut me off!"
But you heard my cry
  when I prayed for help.

Love the Lord, all faithful people,
  the Lord your guardian,
  who fully repays the proud.
Be strong, be brave,
  all who wait for God.

—silence—

PSALM PRAYER

Great God of love: As we walk with Christ throughout this Lent, we seek to reclaim the significance of our baptism. Like the disciples who concluded too soon that Christ had been cut off, we too often assume we know the ending before the story is finished. Teach us to live in hope, that we may be plunged by grace into your Paschal mystery. In the name of Jesus Christ we pray. **Amen.**

Psalm 68

God rises up,
  enemies of heaven scatter:
they disperse like smoke,
  they melt like wax,
  they perish before God.
But the just are glad,
  they rejoice before God
  and celebrate with song.

Sing to God's name, play hymns!
God rides the clouds. Send up a song!
"Lord" is God's name. Rejoice!
Father to the fatherless,
   defender of widows:
   God in the temple!

God gives the homeless a home,
   sets prisoners free to prosper,
   but the rebellious
   are banished to the wild.
God, when you led your people,
   when you marched in the desert,
   earth shook, heaven rained before you,
   Israel's God, the Lord of Sinai.

You gave us downpours
   to refresh the promised land
   where you nourish your flock.
Gracious God, you strengthen the weak.
God speaks a word;
   a company of women
   spreads the good news.

Kings and their armies
   run and flee.
Housewives and shepherds
   all share the plunder:
   silver plated doves
   with bright gold wings.
The Almighty blew kings about
   like snow on Mount Zalmon.

Bashan is a sacred peak,
   a mountain of high summits.
Soaring Bashan, why envy
   the mountain God chose as home,
   a place to live for ever?
With thousands and thousands
   of uncounted chariots
   the Lord came from Sinai
   to Zion's holy temple.

You ascended to the heights,
   you took captives
   and accepted tribute
   from those resisting you.

Bless the Lord each day
   who carries our burden,
   who keeps us alive,
   our God who saves,
   our escape from death.

God smashed the heads of enemies,
   the skulls of the guilty.
The Lord said:
   "I bring them back from Bashan,
   back from the bottom of the sea,
   so you may tramp through their blood
   and your dogs lap it up."

People watched the procession
   as you marched into your house,
   my Lord, my sovereign God.
Singers at the head, musicians at the rear,
   between them, women striking tambourines.

Bless God in the assembly,
   all who draw water
   from Israel's spring.
Little Benjamin leads the princes
   of Judah, Zebulun, and Naphtali.

Use your strength, God,
   as you did for us in the past
   from your house above Jerusalem.
May rulers bring you gifts!

Rebuke the beast of the Nile,
   wild bulls and their calves.
Trample those who lust for silver,
   scatter the war - mongers.

Envoys will come from Egypt,
   the Cushites will pray to God.

Rulers of earth, sing to God.
Make music for the Lord
  who rides the clouds,
  whose voice is thunder.
Acknowledge the power of God
  who governs Israel,
  whose strength is in the storm clouds.
You inspire wonder
  in your temple, God of Israel,
  as you fill your people
  with power and might.
Blessed be God!

—silence—

PSALM PRAYER

Once again, O God, we wait for you to speak your living word, and to hear a company of women spreading the good news. In the midst of our coming celebration, we recognize that there will still be parts of ourselves which have not yet discovered the implications of our baptism, investing you with bloodthirsty vengence rather than saving love. Penetrate us through and through with your transforming grace that we may celebrate with joy and love and peace. In the name of him whose mark we bear, ever Jesus the Christ. **Amen.**

PRAYER OF HEALING AND FORGIVENESS: THE LORD'S PRAYER
(see p. 248)[*]

CANTICLE OF ASSURANCE

Give thanks to the Father,
who made us fit
for the holy community of light
and rescued us from darkness,
bringing us into the realm
of his beloved Son
who redeemed us,
forgiving our sins.

Christ is an image
of the God we cannot see.
Christ is firstborn in all creation.

---

[*] The use of The Lord's Prayer as a prayer of healing and forgiveness is a gift to us from the Benedictines of St. John's Abbey, Collegeville, Minnesota.

Through Christ the universe was made,
things seen and unseen,
thrones, authorities, forces, powers.
Everything was created
through Christ and for Christ.

Before anything came to be, Christ was,
and the universe is held together by Christ.
Christ is also head of the body, the Church,
its beginning as firstborn from the dead,
to become in all things first.

For by God's good pleasure
Christ encompasses
the full measure of power,
reconciling creation with its source
and making peace by the blood of the cross.

(Colossians 1:12-20 ICEL)

GOING FORTH

May God make us worthy of our calling, by whose power every good resolve and work of faith may be fulfilled, so that the name of our Lord Jesus may be glorified in us, and we in him, according to the grace our God and the Lord Jesus Christ. **Amen.**

(Adapted from 2 Thessalonians 1:11-13)
[PRAYERS IN THIS OFFICE: DWV]

Collects and Lessons for Saints' and Martyrs' Days

(to replace morning prayers, concluding collects and scripture lessons)

Readings and Prayers for February 24
St. Matthias the Apostle
Color: Red

Almighty God, you chose Matthias to be numbered among the Twelve. Deliver your church from false apostles and give it faithful and true pastors; through your Son Jesus Christ our Lord. Amen.

[LUTHERAN BOOK OF WORSHIP, ADAPTED; WPM]

LESSONS
Acts 1: 15-26
Psalm 15 (*UMH* 747)
Philippians 3:13-21
John 15:1, 6-16

Gift-giving God, as you guided the Church to see in Matthias the calling of an apostle, so call forth and make evident your gifts in all your people that together we who have become witnesses to your redemption may carry on the work of Christ's apostles, in the power of your Holy Spirit. **Amen.**

[CFG]

Grower of the vineyard, when the vine was injured you strengthened it and grafted Matthias among the Twelve: Always grant us such pastors and leaders that the whole may grow and bear good fruit in Christ. **Amen.**

[CFG]

Readings and Prayers for March 2
John Wesley
Color: White

O God, who plucked as a brand from the burning your servant John Wesley that he might kindle the flame of love in our hearts and illuminate our minds: Grant us such a warming of our hearts that we, being set afire by holy love, may spread its flame to the uttermost parts of the earth, through Jesus Christ our Lord. **Amen.**

[J. E. Rattenbury, alt. CFG]

LESSONS
Isaiah 49:1-6
Psalm 98 (*UMH* 818)
Romans 12:9-20
Luke 9:2-6

Almighty God, who raised up your servant John Wesley to proclaim anew the gift of redemption and the life of holiness: Be with us his children, and revive your work among us; that inspired by the same faith and upheld by the same grace in Word and Sacrament, we and all you people may be made one in the unity of your Church on earth, even as in heaven we are made one in you; through Jesus Christ our Lord, who lives and reigns with you and the Holy Spirit, one God, in glory everlasting. **Amen.**

[Methodist Sacramental Fellowship, alt. TJC]

O almighty God, who in a time of great need raised up your servants John and Charles Wesley, and by your Spirit inspired them to kindle a flame of sacred love which leaped and ran, an inextinguishable blaze: Grant, we ask you, that all those whose hearts have been warmed at these altar fires, being continually refreshed by your grace, may be so devoted that in this our time of great need, your will may fully and effectively be done on earth as it is in heaven; through Jesus Christ our Lord. **Amen.**

[Book of Offices and Services]

Readings and Prayers for March 19:
St. Joseph

O God, who from the family of your servant David raised up Joseph
to be the guardian of your incarnate Son and the spouse of his virgin
mother: Give us grace to imitate his uprightness of life and his obedience to your commands; through Jesus Christ our Lord, who lives
and reigns with you and the Holy Spirit, one God, for ever and ever.
Amen.

[BCP, 239]

LESSONS
2 Samuel 7: 4, 8-16
Psalm 89: 1-29
Romans 4: 13-18
Luke 2: 41-52

Gracious God, by the holy example of Joseph you have drawn us
more deeply into the mystery of your way with the world: Grant that
as living members of the family of saints we might be made perfect in
love and join their ceaseless life of praise, through Jesus Christ our
Lord, who lives and reigns with you and the Holy Spirit, one God,
from generation to generation. **Amen.**

[CFG]

Witnesses in faith, in prayer, and in deed,
holy in life, perfected in love,
with us on earth, around us in heaven,
your faithful saints point to the Way:
    Praise be to God, for the memory of Joseph,
    and for saints who are with us, even today. **Amen.**

[RBA]

March 25
The Annunciation
Color: White
(*Note: When this feast falls on the days of Holy week or of Easter week, it is transferred to the week following the Second Sunday of Easter.*)

Solemn Vespers
For The Feast Of The Annunciation

ENTRANCE OF THE LIGHT
   Light and peace in Jesus Christ!
      Thanks be to God!

   Today is the beginning of our salvation,
   And the manifestation of the mystery from the ages;
      For the Son of God becomes Son of a virgin.
   Therefore, with Gabriel and with Mary, we exult with
   exceedingly great joy:
      For God has regarded the low estate of God's handmaiden.
   From day to day show forth the salvation of our God.
      Sing aloud to God a new song.
      [ADAPTED FROM THE "TROPARION AND PROKEIMENON OF MATINS FOR ANNUNCIATION DAY" IN THE BOOK OF DIVINE
      PRAYERS AND SERVICES OF THE CATHOLIC ORTHODOX CHURCH OF CHRIST; WPM]

HYMN OF LIGHT (The *"Phos hilaron;"* see cover 2)

THANKSGIVING FOR LIGHT
   Blessed are you, God of all grace,
      for in Jesus Christ, you are our light and our life;
      to you be glory and praise forever!
   You gave your living Word to Mary, Birth-Giver,
      that through the Holy Spirit
      she might bear the Word made flesh,
      who brings life out of darkness,
      and with your Spirit renews the face of the earth.
   All thanks and praise to you,
      Most holy and blessed Trinity,
      One God, now and forever. **Amen.**

                                                                          [DWV]

INCENSE
[during the singing of the Evening Prayer Canticle, candles may be lit and incense placed before an icon of Mary as a sign of the presence of the Holy Spirit and the prayers of the whole people of God.]

EVENING PRAYER CANTICLE (selected from Psalm 141)
CHANT FORM (*see Cover 2*)
METRICAL FORM (*see page 2*)

PRAYER OF THE DAY
Almighty God, who sent the angel Gabriel to the virgin Mary and
through her obedience and faith brought forth your Son: Grant that
we too may remain receptive to your visitation and believe the word
you speak to us, through Jesus Christ our Lord, who lives and reigns
with you and the Holy Spirit, one God, now and forever. **Amen.**
[DTB]

FIRST READING Isaiah 7:10-14

INVITATORY AND PSALTER
O God, come to our assistance.
O Lord, hasten to help us.
Glory to you, O Trinity, most holy and blessed;
One God, now and forever. Amen.

Psalm 87

Zion is set on the ho-ly *mountain.*
The Lord loves her gates
    above all the dwellings of *Israel.*
Great is your renown, city of *God.*
I register as her citizens
    Egypt and Babylon,
    Philistia, Ethiopia, and Tyre:
"Each one was born in *her.*"

People will say, "Zion mothered
    each and ev-ery *one.*"
The Most High pro-tects the *city.*
God records in the register,
    "This one was *born here.*"
Then people will dance and sing,
    "My home is *here!*"

THE GLORIA (*see cover 3; musical setting,* UMH 72)
Glory to God, Love abounding be-fore all *ages;*
Glory to God, Love shown forth in the self-emptying of Je-sus *Christ;*
Glory to God, Love poured out through the gift of the *Spirit,*
    who fashions and renews the face of the *earth;*

Glory to the holy and <u>bless</u>-ed *Trinity!*
All things abiding in Love,
  Love abiding <u>in</u> all *things,*
As it is now, <u>ev</u>-er *was,*
And ever shall be for endless ages. <u>A</u>-*men.*

[DNP]

SECOND READING   Hebrews 10:4-10

GOSPEL READING   Luke 1:26-38

—silent reflection—

CANTICLE OF MARY (The *Magnificat;* Luke 1:39-56):
  (see *UMH* 198-200, and Stanza 4 of 197 for metrical versions)

Chant Form A (*see Cover 2*)
Chant Form B (*see page 4*)

READINGS FOR MEDITATION AND REFLECTION

PRAYERS
  God of vision and dream, our world and experience are not porous
  to your strange stirrings. By your Holy Spirit, make our hearts and
  minds penetrable like Mary's, and conceive Christ in our imagina-
  tions, hopes and habits. Amen.

[DTB]

  Hear us as we pray
  for all who hear your word of grace . . .
  that we may be open to the power of your word within us . . .
  that through the power of your Holy Spirit
    we may bear that word to others . . .
  that we may join our prayers with all your people
    for those in special need of your healing
    and empowering presence,
    whom we name now before you . . .

[DWV]

Silent Prayer

[Other selected prayers (*from the following or other resources*)

The Collect for Peace
  Most holy God, the source of all good desires, all right judgements,
  and all just works; Give to us, your servants, that peace which the

world cannot give, so that our minds may be fixed on the doing of your will, and the fear of our enemies having been removed, we may pass our time in rest and quietness; Through the mercies of Jesus Christ our Savior. **Amen.**

[Gelasian Sacramentary, 8th Century, Alt. TJC]

The Collect for Aid Against Perils

O God, the life of all who live, the light of the faithful, the strength of those who labor, and the repose of the dead: We thank you for the blessings of the day that is past and humbly ask for your protection through the coming night. Bring us in safety to the morning hours; Through him who died and rose again for us, our Savior Jesus Christ. **Amen.**

[Mozarabic Sacramentary, 6th Century; Alt. TJC]

Prayers of Special intention *(such as the following)*:
[Intercessions for the Order of Saint Luke *(see cover 3)*
[A Collect for the Order of Saint Luke *(see p. 248)*

Concluding Collect

Lord God, in the mystery of the incarnation, you chose Mary to bear your son. Grant that we may show forth the mystery of your love in our lifelong pilgrimage to his cross and resurrection, and so bear Jesus' love to the world; who lives and reigns with you and the holy Spirit, one God forever. **Amen.**

[Catholic Orthodox Church of Christ, WPM]

The Lord's Prayer *(see p. 248)*
(See UMH 270-271 for musical settings)

HYMN [LM; Tune: CONDITOR ALME, *UMH* 692]
The God whom earth and sea and sky
adore and laud and magnify,
whose might they own, whose praise they tell,
in Mary's body deigned to dwell.

O Mother blest! The chosen shrine
wherein the architect divine,
whose hand contains the earth and sky,
vouchsafed in hidden guise to lie:

Blest in the message Gabriel brought;
blest in the work the Spirit wrought;
most blest, to bring to human birth
the long Desired of all the earth.

O Lord, the Virgin-born to thee
eternal praise and glory be,
whom with the Father we adore
and Holy Spirit evermore.

[BISHOP VENANTIUS FORTUNATUS (c.530-c.600),
TRANS. JOHN MASON NEALE 1818-1866]

When the office of Compline is not prayed, the Commendation Prayer and the Canticle of Simeon (see pages 10-11) are included here.

GOING FORTH

May the God of hope fill us all with joy and peace in believing, so that we may abound in hope by the power of the Holy Spirit.

(Romans 15:13 alt.)

Let us bless the Lord.
Thanks be to God.

March 29
Charles Wesley
Color: White

Genesis 32:22-32
Psalm 96 (*UMH* 815)
Colossians 3:12-17
Matthew 26:26-30

Almighty and passionate God, the source of all seers and poets who give expression to the deep mystery of faith, you inspired Charles Wesley to pour out his love for you in his vocation as poet, pastor, and preacher: Grant, that continually encouraged by his hymns and example, we too may rise up to be faithful followers of Jesus Christ our Lord, who lives and reigns with you and the Holy Spirit, one God, now and forever. **Amen.**

[DTB AND CFG]

Anointing Spirit whose grace is ever fresh in the songs and hymns of the church: pour out your dreams and visions upon us in worship and devotion that we may do justice and act with compassion for the poor and oppressed through Christ, our Lord. **Amen.**

[DTB]

Propers of the Day

for

Lent

Evening Prayer

For the Evening before Ash Wednesday

ENTRANCE OF THE LIGHT
Light and peace in Jesus Christ.
Thanks be to God!
Come, my Light, my Feast, my Strength:
Such a Light, as shows a feast:
Such a Feast, as mends in length:
Such a Strength, as makes us guests.

[GEORGE HERBERT, 1593-1633]

HYMN OF LIGHT: (*The "Phos hilaron," see front cover*)

THANKSGIVING FOR THE LIGHT
Our Lord and God: with your light enlighten the movements of our meditations that we may hear and understand the sweet listenings to your life-giving commands; and grant that through your grace and mercy we may gather from them the assurance of love, and hope, and salvation, and we shall sing to you everlasting glory without ceasing and always, O God of all. **Amen.**

(LITURGY OF THE BLESSED APOSTLES, 5TH c.TAR)

EVENING PRAYER CANTICLE (*see front cover*)

CONFESSION AND PARDON
Almighty and eternal God, who drew out a fountain of living water in the desert for your people, draw from the hardness of our hearts tears of compunction, that we may be able to lament our sins, and receive you in your mercy.   (LATIN, LATE 14TH C.)

—silent confession—

If we confess our sins, God is faithful and just, and will forgive our sins and cleanse us from all unrighteousness. In Christ, we are forgiven.
Thanks be to God.

PSALTER Psalm 36

I

Sin whispers <u>with</u> the *wicked,*
shares its evil, <u>heart</u> to *heart.*
These sinners shut their eyes
    to all <u>fear</u> of *God.*
They refuse to see their sin,
    to <u>know it</u> and *hate it.*

Their words ring <u>false</u> and *empty,*
their plans ne - <u>glect</u> what is *good.*
They <u>daydream</u> of *evil,*
plot their crooked ways,
    seizing on <u>all</u> that is *vile.*

II

Your mercy, Lord, <u>spans</u> the *sky;*
your faithfulness soars a-<u>mong</u> the *clouds.*
Your integrity towers <u>like</u> a *mountain;*
your justice runs deeper <u>than</u> the *sea.*

Lord, you em-<u>brace</u> all *life:*
How we prize your <u>ten</u>-der *mercy!*
God, your <u>people</u> seek *shelter,*
safe in the <u>warmth</u> of your *wings.*

They feast at <u>your</u> full *table,*
slake their thirst in <u>your</u> cool *stream,*
for you are the <u>fount</u> of *life,*
you give us <u>light</u> and we *see.*

III

Grant mercy always <u>to</u> your *own,*
victory to <u>hon</u>-est *hearts.*
Keep the proud from trampling me,
    assaulting me with <u>wick</u>-ed *hands.*
Let those sinners collapse,
    struck down, <u>never</u> to *rise.*

THE GLORIA (*see back cover; musical setting, UMH 72; or:*)
  Glory to God, Love abounding be-<u>fore</u> all *ages;*
  Glory to God, Love shown forth in the self-emptying of <u>Je</u>-sus *Christ;*
  Glory to God, Love poured out through the <u>gift</u> of the *Spirit,*
    who fashions and renews the <u>face</u> of the *earth;*
  Glory to the holy and <u>bless</u>-ed *Trinity!*
  All things abiding in Love,
    Love abiding <u>in</u> all *things,*
  As it is now, <u>ev</u>-er *was,*
  and ever shall be for endless ages. <u>A</u>-*men.*

[DNP]

SCRIPTURE(S) Philippians 2:1-13
                John 18:15-18, 25-27
                    —*silent reflection*—

CANTICLE OF MARY (*see front cover*)

[READING(S) FOR MEDITATION AND REFLECTION

PRAYERS

PRAYERS OF THANKSGIVING AND INTERCESSION
Our new Moses: you led us through the sea
  and trampled down our ancient foes.
In baptism you pierced our hardness of heart
  And engraved your law within us.
Blessed are you! Holy! Worthy! Matchless!
In the coming days of Lent,
  prepare us to be plunged anew
  into your Paschal Mystery,
  renewing the baptismal covenant
  that marks us as your own.
Save us and all your daughters and sons
  from going back to lust for our old way of life.
Heal all who cry out to you in suffering.
Hear and deliver the oppressed in their anguish and misery.
Surround seekers and catechumens with soul-friends.
Befriend penitents with hope and merciful encouragers.
Receive those we let down through the roof
  for your touch this night . . .

[DTB, DWV]

—silent prayer—

[OTHER SELECTED PRAYERS (*see page 4ff*)

[PRAYERS OF SPECIAL INTENTION (*such as the following*)
  [INTERCESSIONS FOR THE ORDER OF SAINT LUKE (*see back cover*)
  [A COLLECT FOR THE ORDER OF SAINT LUKE (*see p. 248*)

CONCLUDING PRAYER
O Lord our God, grant us grace to desire you with our whole heart,
that so desiring, we may seek and find you. and so finding you we
may love you; and loving you we may hate those sins from which
you have redeemed us; for the sake of Jesus Christ. **Amen.**

(ST. ANSELM, 1033-1109)

THE LORD'S PRAYER
(*See p. 248; see* UMH 270-271 *for musical settings*)

HYMN   (87.87.87; Tune: LAUDA ANIMA, *UMH* 100)
[This hymn is appropriate as our singing of "alleluia" is put away for Lent]

Alleluia, song of gladness, voice of joy that cannot die;
alleluia is the anthem ever dear to choirs on high;
in the house of God abiding they lift up their joyful cry.

Alleluia, now resounding, true Jerusalem and free;
alleluia, joyful mother, all your children sing with thee;
but by Babylon's sad waters, mourning exiles we shall be.

Alleluia cannot always be our song while here below;
alleluia, our transgressions make us for a while give o'er;
for the holy time is coming when our tears for sin must flow.

Therefore in our hymns we pray thee, grant us, blessed Trinity,
at the last to keep your Easter, with your saints eternally,
there to you forever singing Alleluia joyfully.

[ELEVENTH CENTURY LATIN HYMN; J. M. NEALE, TRANS. ALT.]

GOING FORTH
We have had feasting and sweetness of milk,
Honey and water, bread and the cup.
We have had harp and psaltry and horn,
Sweet psaltry music and alleluias.

Now the High King of heaven,
And Jesus the Christ,
And the Spirit of peace and of grace be with us.
Amen and amen!

[ADAPTED FROM A CELTIC BLESSING ON ASH EVE, DWV]

Let us bless the Lord. Alleluia!
Thanks be to God! Alleluia!

(here as a silent, symbolic gesture, a banner or scroll with the word "ALLE-LUIA" may be put away. We will not sing or hear it again until we sing it during the Great Paschal Vigil at Easter.)

Vígíl

For the night before Ash Wednesday

(This service may be prayed as a solitary or corporate office on Ash Wednesday, replacing the mid-morning, mid-day, or mid-afternoon office.)

CALL TO PRAYER
O Lord, open my lips,
And my mouth shall proclaim your praise.
O God, come to my assistance.
O Lord, hasten to help me.

CANTICLE OF REDEMPTION (*De Profundis*)
[Psalm Tune Five (for a metrical form, see *UMH* 515)]

Out of the depths I cry to you, O God;
Lord, <u>hear</u> my *voice.*
Incline your ear to the voice of my <u>sup</u>-pli-*cation.*
If you were to mark all iniquities,
O God, <u>who</u> could *stand?*
But there is forgiveness with you
that you <u>may</u> be *worshiped.*

I wait for the Lord, <u>my</u> soul *waits,*
and in God's <u>word</u> I *hope;*
My soul waits for the Lord
more than those who watch <u>for</u> the *morning;*
more than those who watch <u>for</u> the *morning.*

O Israel, trust <u>in</u> the *Lord;*
with God there is mercy and plent-<u>eous</u> re-*demption*
for the Lord will redeem <u>Is</u>-ra-*el*
from <u>all</u> in-*iquities.*

(Psalm 30; alt DWV)

THE BLESSING
Lord, grant us your blessing.
May God light the fire of divine love in our hearts.   Amen.

THE PSALTER
[Note: the readings for this office emphasize our sin and mortality and are all taken from the Psalter; each reading is followed by a time of silence.]

Psalm 5

I

Solo 1:   Hear my words, my groans,
             my cries for help,
             O God my king.
           I pray to you, Lord,
             my prayer rises with the sun.
           At dawn I plead my case and wait.

II

Solo 2:   You never welcome evil, God,
             never let it stay.
           You hate arrogance
             and abhor scoundrels,
             you detest violence
             and destroy the traitor.

III

Unison: But by your great mercy
             I enter your house
             and bend low in awe
             within your holy temple.

           In the face of my enemies
             clear the way,
             bring me your justice.

Solo 1:   Their charges are groundless,
             they breathe destruction;
           their tongues are smooth,
             their throat an open grave.

Solo 2:   God, pronounce them guilty,
             catch them in their own plots,
             expel them for their sins;
             they have betrayed you.

IV

Unison: But let those who trust you
             be glad and celebrate for ever.
           Protect those who love your name,
             then they will delight in you.

           For you bless the just, O God,
             your grace surrounds them like a shield.
                    —*silence*—

Psalm 22

Solo 1: God, my God,
    why have you abandoned me-
    far from my cry, my words of pain?
I call by day, you do not answer;
I call by night, but find no rest.

Solo 2: You are the Holy One enthroned,
    the Praise of Israel.
Our people trusted, they trusted you;
you rescued them.
To you they cried, and they were saved;
they trusted and were not shamed.

Solo 1: But I am a worm, hardly human,
    despised by all, mocked by the crowd.
All who see me jeer at me,
    sneer at me, shaking their heads:
"You relied on God; let God help you!
If God loves you, let God save you!"

Solo 2: But you, God, took me from the womb,
    you kept me safe at my mother's breast.
I belonged to you from the time of birth,
    you are my God from my mother's womb.

Choir 1: Do not stay far off,
    danger is so close.
I have no other help.
Wild bulls surround me,
    bulls of Bashan encircle me,
    opening their jaws against me
    like roaring, ravening lions.

Choir 2: I am poured out like water,
    my bones are pulled apart,
    my heart is wax melting within me,
    my throat baked and dry,
    my tongue stuck to my jaws.
You bring me down to the dust of death.

Choir 1: There are dogs all around me,
    a pack of villains corners me.

They tear at my hands and feet,
  I can count all my bones.
They stare at me and gloat.
They take what I wore,
  they roll dice for my clothes.

Choir 2:   Lord, do not stay far off,
  you, my strength, be quick to help.
Save my neck from the sword,
  save my life from the dog's teeth,
  save me from the lion's jaws,
  save me from the bull's horns.

You hear me.

II

Unison: I will proclaim your name to my people,
I will praise you in the assembly.

Give praise, all who fear God:
  revere and honor the Lord,
  children of Israel, people of Jacob.
The Lord never scorns the afflicted,
  never looks away, but hears their cry.

Choir 1:   I will sing of you in the great assembly,
  make good my promise before your faithful.
The poor shall eat all they want.
Seekers of God shall give praise.
"May your hearts live for ever!"

Choir 2:   All peoples shall remember and turn,
  all races will bow to the Lord,
  who holds dominion over nations.
The well-fed crowd kneel before God,
  all destined to die bow low.

Unison: My soul lives for the Lord!
My children will serve,
  will proclaim God to the future,
  announcing to peoples yet unborn,
"God saves."

—*silence*—

Psalm 25 (chanted)

I

Lord, I give my-<u>self</u> to *you.*
I <u>trust</u> you, *God;*
   do not fail me, nor let my <u>ene</u>-mies *gloat.*
No one loyal is shamed,
   but traitors <u>know</u> dis-*grace.*

Teach me <u>how</u> to *live,*
Lord, show <u>me</u> the *way.*
Steer me t<u>oward</u> your *truth,*
   you, my saving God,
   you, my <u>con</u>-stant *hope.*

Recall your tenderness,
   your <u>last</u>-ing *love.*
Remember me, not my faults,
   the sins <u>of</u> my *youth.*
To show <u>your</u> own *goodness,*
   God, re-<u>mem</u>-ber *me.*

II

Good and just is the Lord,
   guiding <u>those</u> who *stray.*
God leads the poor,
   pointing <u>out</u> the *path.*
God's ways are faithful love
   for those who <u>keep</u> the *covenant.*
Be true to your name, O Lord,
   forgive my <u>sin</u>, though *great.*

Do you respect God?
   Then God will <u>guide</u> your *choice.*
Your life will be full,
   your heirs will <u>keep</u> the *land.*
God be-<u>friends</u> the *faithful,*
teaches <u>them</u> the *covenant.*

III

I keep looking to God
   to spring me <u>from</u> this *trap.*
Turn, treat me as your friend,
   I am <u>empty</u> and *poor.*

Release my trapped heart,
   free me <u>from</u> my *anguish*.
See my misery, my pain,
   take my <u>sins</u> a-*way*.

See how they mob me,
   this crowd that hates me.
   Protect me and <u>save</u> my *life*.
Keep me from disgrace,
   for I take <u>shelter</u> in *you*.
Let integrity stand guard
   as I <u>wait</u> for *you*.
Free Israel, O God,
   from <u>all</u> its *troubles*

—silence—

Psalm 39

I

Solo 1:   I said I will not sin!
             I will curb my tongue
                and muzzle my mouth
                   when the wicked confront me.

             I kept silent,
                would not say a word,
                yet my anguish grew.
             It scorched my heart
                and seared my thoughts
                until I had to speak.

II

Solo 2:   Lord, what will become of me?
             How long will I live?
             Let me see how short life is!

             You give me a brief span of time;
                before you, my days are nothing.
             People are but a breath:
                they walk like shadows;
                their efforts amount to nothing;
                they hoard, but others gain.

Solo 1:   Why do I wait for you, Lord?
You are my hope
  to save me from my sins;
  do not make a fool of me.
I will keep quiet.
I have said enough,
  since all this is your doing.

Solo 2:   Stop tormenting me;
  you strike and I grow weak.
You rebuke us for our sin,
  eat up our riches like a moth;
  we are but a breath.

Unison: Lord, hear my prayer,
  my cry for help.
Do not ignore my tears,
  as if I were alien to you,
  a stranger like my ancestors.
Stop looking so hard at me,
allow me a little joy
before I am no more.

—silence—

Psalm 40 (*chanted*)

I

I waited and <u>waited</u> for *God.*
At long last God bent down
  to <u>hear</u> my com-*plaint,*
and pulled me from the grave
  <u>out of</u> the *swamp,*
and gave me a steady stride
  on <u>rock</u>-solid *ground.*

God taught me a new song,
  a <u>hymn</u> of *praise.*
Seeing all this,
  many will be moved
  to <u>trust</u> in the *Lord.*
Happy are they who <u>trust</u> in *God,*
not seduced by idols
  nor won <u>over</u> by *lies.*

You do so many wonders,
   you show you care for us,
   <u>Lord</u> my *God;*
you are beyond compare;
   Were I to name them all,
   no one <u>could</u> keep *track.*
You did not seek offerings
   or <u>ask</u> for *sacrifices;*
but you drilled ears
   for <u>me</u> to *hear.*

"Yes," I said, "I will come
   to live by your <u>writ</u>-ten *word."*
I want to do what pleases you;
   your teaching is <u>in</u> my *heart.*
I celebrate your justice
   before <u>all</u> the as-*sembly;*
I do not hold back the story.
   Lord, you know <u>this</u> is *true.*

I did not hide in my heart
   your <u>acts</u> of *rescue;*
I boldly declared to all
   your truth and care, your <u>faith</u>-ful *love.*
Your maternal love
   sur-<u>rounds</u> me, *Lord.*
Your sure and tender care
   pro-<u>tects</u> me *always.*

II

Countless <u>evils</u> sur-*round me,*
more than the hairs <u>on</u> my *head;*
my sins overwhelm me,
   so many I can <u>hard</u>-ly *see.*
My courage <u>fails</u> - *me.*

Please, <u>Lord -</u> , *rescue me;*
hurry, <u>Lord -</u> , *help me.*
Stop my killers, shame them,
   wipe out my <u>bit</u>-ter *enemies.*
Let those who jeer at me,
   "Too bad for you!"
   be re-<u>warded</u> with *shame.*

But let all who seek you
    and <u>count</u> on your *strength*
sing and dance and cheer
    "<u>Glory</u> to *God!*"
Though I am weak and poor,
    God <u>cares</u> for *me.*
My help, my savior,
    my <u>God,</u> act *now!*

—*silence*—

Psalm 42

I

Solo 1:   As a deer craves running water,
        I thirst for you, my God;
    I thirst for God,
        the living God.
    When will I see your face?

    Tears are my steady diet.
    Day and night I hear,
    "Where is your God?"

    I cry my heart out,
        I remember better days:
    when I entered the house of God,
        I was caught in the joyful sound
        of pilgrims giving thanks.

Unison: Why are you sad, my heart?
    Why do you grieve?
    Wait for the Lord.
    I will yet praise God my savior.

II

Solo 2:   My heart is sad.
    Even from Jordan and Hermon,
        from the peak of Mizar,
        I remember you.

    There the deep roars to deep;
    your torrents crash over me.
    The love God summoned by day
    sustained my praise by night,
    my prayer to the living God.

I complain to God,
   who I thought was rock:
"Why have you forgotten me?
Why am I bent double
   under the weight of enemies?

"Their insults grind me to dust.
Day and night they say,
   'Where is your God?'"

Unison: Why are you sad, my heart?
Why do you grieve?
Wait for the Lord.
I will yet praise God my savior.

—silence—

RESPONSORY Hosea 6:1-3

Let us return to the Lord
   who tore us apart
but now will heal us;
   who struck us down
   yet binds our wounds;
who revives us after two days,
   raising us up on the third,
   to live in God's presence.

Let us seek to know the Lord,
   whose coming is sure as dawn,
   who descends like the rain,
   spring rain renewing the earth.

COLLECT
Righteous God: In the sacrifice of Christ you show your love for us.
Help us admit to ourselves that we have often rejected your love with
disdain. Forgive our sin, that we may reach with confidence for your
mercy; through the same Jesus Christ our Redeemer. **Amen.**

[GLH]

THE LORD'S PRAYER (*see p. 248*)

CONCLUDING PRAYERS

O Lord, hear my prayer,
  And let my cry come to you.
Listen to the prayers of your servants;
  have mercy on us, Lord Jesus Christ.
Let us bless the Lord.
  Thanks be to God!

[ADAPTED FROM THE ROMAN BREVIARY]

Morning Prayer

For Ash Wednesday

CALL TO PRAYER

    O Lord, open my lips
      and my mouth shall proclaim your praise.
    Return to me, says the LORD of hosts,
    and I will return to you.

(Zechariah 1:3)

HYMN [LM; Tune: WAREHAM, *UMH* 258]

This fast, as taught by holy lore,
we keep in solemn course once more;
this Lenten fast is known and bound
in forty days each yearly round.

In prayer together let us fall
and cry for mercy, one and all,
and weep before the Judge's feet
and God's forgiving love entreat.

Forgive the sin that we have wrought,
increase the good that we have sought,
that we at length, our wanderings o'er,
may please You here and evermore.

Grant, O most blessed Trinity,
grant, O Essential Unity,
that this our fast for forty days
may work our profit and Your praise.

[TRADITIONAL DAILY OFFICE HYMN, ALT. DTB AND DWV]

MORNING PRAYER

    Almighty and everlasting God: You hate nothing you have made and forgive the sins of all who are penitent. Create in us new and contrite hearts, that we, lamenting our sins and acknowledging our separation, may receive your forgiveness and by your Spirit be renewed in our baptism, through Jesus Christ our Lord. **Amen.**

[BCP ALT]

PSALTER Psalm 102

I

Hear my prayer, Lord,
    let my <u>cry</u>- *reach you.*
Do not turn from me
    in my <u>hour</u> of *need.*

When I call, listen,
   answer <u>me</u> at *once.*
For my days dissolve like smoke,
   my bones are <u>burned</u> to *ash.*

My heart withers a-<u>way</u> like *grass.*
I even forget to eat,
   so consumed am I with grief.
   My skin hangs <u>on</u> my *bones.*
Like a gull lost in the desert,
   like an owl <u>haunting</u> the *ruins,*
I keep a solitary watch,
   a lone bird <u>on</u> a *roof.*

All day my enemies mock me,
   they make my <u>name</u> a *curse.*
For bread, I eat ashes,
   tears <u>salt</u> my *drink.*
You lifted me up in anger
   and threw me <u>to</u> the *ground.*
My days pass into evening,
   I wither <u>like</u> the *grass.*

II

But you, Lord, preside for ever,
   every <u>age</u> re-*members you.*
Rise with mercy for Zion,
   for now is the <u>time</u> for *pity.*
Your servants treasure <u>ev'ry</u> *stone,*
   they cherish <u>even</u> the *rubble.*

Nations will fear your name,
   your glory will <u>hum</u>-ble *kings.*
When you rebuild Zion's walls,
   you will appear in <u>glo</u>-ry, *Lord.*
You hear the <u>home</u>-less *pleading*
and do not <u>mock</u> their *prayer.*

Write this down for those to come,
   a people created to <u>praise</u> our *God:*
"The Lord watches from on high,
   searches the <u>earth</u> from *heaven.*

God hears the prisoner's groan
   and sets the doomed free
   to sing the Lord's name in Zion,
   God's <u>praise</u> in Je-*rusalem.*
There the nations and peoples
   gather to <u>serve</u> the *Lord."*

III

God has broken me in my prime,
   has cut <u>short</u> my *days.*
I say: "My God, do not take me.
   My life is only half-spent,
   while you live from <u>age</u> to *age."*
Long ago you made the earth,
   the heavens, too, <u>are</u> your *work.*
Should they decay, <u>you</u> re-*main.*

Should they wear out like a robe,
   like clothing changed and <u>thrown</u> a-*way,*
   you are still the same.
Your years will <u>nev</u>-er *end.*
May your servants' line <u>last</u> for *ever,*
   our children grow <u>strong</u> be-*fore you.*

THE GLORIA *(see back cover)*

SCRIPTURE

—silent reflection—

CANTICLE OF ZECHARIAH *(see back cover or p.16)*

[READING(S) FOR MEDITATION AND REFLECTION]

[INVITATION TO THE OBSERVANCE OF LENTEN DISCIPLINE]

[IMPOSITION OF ASHES]　　　*(See denominational resources,*
　　　　　　　　　　　　　　such as UMBOW, *p. 322)*

PRAYERS

PRAYERS OF THANKSGIVING AND SUPPLICATION
Purifying Mystery, your light exposes in us all that we hide.
Awaken us and all your Holy Church to spiritual combat.

Lead us to purity of soul and body in these forty days.
Fortify us to take an honest look at our selves
    and to name our secret sins and our ruts of disobedience.
Let abstinence from our addictions free us for prayer
    and the fire of love.
Perfect us by steady gaze toward your pure mercy and grace
    so we may come to the Passion of Jesus and the
    Holy Pascha in pure joy.
In confidence we commend ourselves and all our passions
    and cares to your never failing mercy.

We intercede for the world and the church:
    especially for those we have hurt by our preoccupations . . .
    for those who live sacrificially so others
        may know your justice and compassion . . .
    for a just peace in and among the nations . . .
    for professionals who help others stand in the light . . .
    for the Church in every place . . .
    for the concerns and cares of our lives . . .

(DTB)

—silent prayer—

[OTHER SELECTED PRAYERS *(see pages 17ff)*

[PRAYERS OF SPECIAL INTENTION *(such as the following)*
    [INTERCESSIONS FOR THE ORDER OF SAINT LUKE *(see back cover)*
    [A COLLECT FOR THE ORDER OF SAINT LUKE *(see p. 248)*

CONCLUDING PRAYER
Holy God, whose spirit drives us into the wilderness to confront our
priorities with a holy fast; grant that as we are about to do battle with
our demons and the power of evil, we may be defended by your grace
through Jesus Christ. **Amen.**

[DTB/DWV]

THE LORD'S PRAYER *(see p. 248)*
    (UMH *270-271 for musical settings*)

HYMN [7777; Tune: CANTERBURY, *UMH* 355]

Forty days and forty nights
You were fasting in the wild;
forty days and forty nights
tempted, and yet undefiled.

Shall not we your sorrow share
and from worldly joys abstain,
fasting with unceasing prayer,
strong with you to suffer pain?

Then if Satan on us press,
flesh or spirit to assail,
victor in the wilderness,
grant that we not faint nor fail!

So shall we have peace divine:
holier gladness ours shall be;
'round us, too, shall angels shine,
such as served you faithfully.

Keep, O keep us, Savior dear,
ever constant by your side;
that with you we may appear
at th'eternal Eastertide.

[GEORGE HUNT SMYTTAN (1856)]

GOING FORTH

Let us lay aside every weight and the sin that clings so closely, and let
us run with perseverance the race that is set before us, looking to Jesus
the pioneer and perfecter of our faith.

(adapted from Hebrews 12: 1-2)

The grace of the Lord Jesus be with us.
Let us bless the Lord.
   Thanks be to God.

Solemn Vespers

For Ash Wednesday

ENTRANCE OF THE LIGHT
O God, come to our assistance.
O Lord, hasten to help us.
My soul yearns for you in the night.
Those who sleep in the dust will awake and shout for joy;
for your dew shines forth with sparkling light,
and the earth will bring those long dead to birth again.

(Isaiah 26:9, 19)

HYMN OF LIGHT (*The "Phos hilaron;" see front cover*)

EVENING PRAYER CANTICLE (*see front cover*)

[INVITATION TO THE OBSERVANCE OF LENTEN DISCIPLINE]

[IMPOSITION OF ASHES]
(*if not included in some other service; See denominational resources such as*
UMBOW, *p. 322*)

CONFESSION AND PARDON
In the dust of isolation and disconnectedness we cry to you, O Lord.
We have loved short-sightedly. We have trusted illusions.
We are left longing and grieving in space
   that turns from grit and dust,
while an angel with whirling sword stands behind us.
Our brows bear the sign of our heart's ashes.
Our life is over like a sigh. In your cross is our only hope.
Come "wash again and ever again this soiled world",
through Christ, our only mediator and advocate.
Amen.

[DTB, THE QUOTE IS FROM A LINE OF WALT WHITMAN]

—*silence*—

"Those who are well have no need of a physician, but those who are
sick; I have come to call not the righteous but sinners to repentance."

(Luke 5:31-32)

PSALTER Psalm 51:1-17
   Have mercy, tender God,
      forget that I de-*fied you.*
   Wash away my sin,
      cleanse me <u>from</u> my *guilt.*

I know my evil well,
  it stares me <u>in</u> the *face,*
evil done to you alone
  before your <u>ve</u>-ry *eyes.*

How right your condemnation!
  Your verdict <u>clear</u>-ly *just.*
You see me for what I am,
  a sinner be-<u>fore</u> my *birth.*
You love those centered in truth;
  teach me your <u>hid</u>-den *wisdom.*
Wash me with fresh water,
  wash me <u>bright</u> as *snow.*

Fill me with happy songs,
  let the bones you <u>bruised</u> now *dance.*
Shut your eyes to my sin,
  make my guilt <u>dis</u>-ap-*pear.*
Creator, reshape my heart,
  God, <u>steady</u> my *spirit.*
Do not cast me aside
  stripped of your <u>ho</u>-ly *spirit.*

Save me, bring <u>back</u> my *joy,*
support me, <u>strengthen</u> my *will.*
Then I will <u>teach</u> your *way*
and sinners will <u>turn</u> to *you.*

Help me, stop my tears,
  and I will <u>sing</u> your *goodness.*
Lord, give me words
  and I will <u>shout</u> your *praise.*

When I offer a holocaust,
  the gift <u>does</u> not *please you.*
So I offer my shattered spirit;
  a changed <u>heart</u> you *welcome.*

—silence—

WORDS OF ASSURANCE
  We are touched and healed by the physician of our souls;
  in the name of Jesus Christ we are forgiven.
    Thanks be to God!

CANTICLE OF REDEMPTION (*De Profundis*)
[Psalm Tune Five (for a metrical form, see *UMH* 515)]

Out of the depths I cry to you, O God;
  Lord, <u>hear</u> my *voice.*
Incline your ear to the voice of my <u>sup</u>-pli-*cation.*
If you were to mark all iniquities,
  O God, <u>who</u> could *stand?*
But there is forgiveness with you
  that you <u>may</u> be *worshiped.*

I wait for the Lord, my soul waits,
  and in God's <u>word</u> *I hope;*
My soul waits for the Lord
  more than those who watch for the morning;
    more than those who watch <u>for</u> the *morning.*

O Israel, trust in the Lord;
  with God there is mercy and <u>plenteous</u> re-*demption*
  for the Lord will redeem Israel from <u>all</u> in-*iquities.*

(Psalm 30; alt DWV)

SCRIPTURES (*see daily lectionary*)

—*silent reflection*—

CANTICLE OF MARY (*see front cover*)

[READING(S) FOR MEDITATION AND REFLECTION

PRAYERS

Prayers of Intercession and Supplication
Enduring God: Your years never come to an end,
  but our days pass away like smoke.
We thank you for these Lenten days when, by holy discipline,
  you say to us:
"Seek me and live — seek good and not evil."
Turn our eyes toward Jesus whose struggle yielded
  the peaceful fruit of righteousness.
Humble us with these ashes in anticipation of your exaltation.
Let outward discipline and inward prayer
  stir the deep hunger and yearning of our hearts
    to turn to you and live.
  Let our turning be genuine and without shortcut.

Let our turning be in mutual accountability
  so we help one another to speak and do the truth.
Let no sin be hidden and all our thirst, blindness and death
  be exposed to your grace.
Bring us all the way home from the far country.
Let this day's ashes mark the beginning of a forty day journey
  that will take the rest of our life.

[DTB]

—silent prayer—

[OTHER SELECTED PRAYERS *(see pages 4ff)*

[PRAYERS OF SPECIAL INTENTION *(such as the following)*
  [INTERCESSIONS FOR THE ORDER OF SAINT LUKE *(see back cover)*
  [A COLLECT FOR THE ORDER OF SAINT LUKE *(see p. 248)*

CONCLUDING PRAYER
God of mercy, who created us from the dust of earth; and claimed us
in Christ through the waters of baptism: Guide us on our pilgrimage
through these desert days that as a baptized people, we may hunger
and thirst for justice and peace, and participate in Christ's dying and
rising. May we live and pray in the name of Jesus. **Amen.**

THE LORD'S PRAYER *(see p. 248)*
  (See UMH 270-271 for musical settings)

HYMN (77.77D; Tune: ABERYSTWYTH, *UMH* 479)

Savior, when in dust to thee
Low we bow th' adoring knee;
when, repentant, to the skies
scarce we lift our weeping eyes;
O by all thy pains and woe
suffered once for all below,
bending from thy throne on high,
hear our solemn litany.

By thy helpless infant years,
by thy life of want and tears,
by thy days of sore distress
in a savage wilderness;
by the dread mysterious hour
of th' insulting tempter's power:
turn, O turn a favoring eye,
hear our solemn litany.

By the sacred griefs that wept
o'er the grave where Lazarus slept;
by the boding tears that flowed
over Salem's loved abode;
by the mournful word that told
treach'ry lurked within thy fold:
From thy seat above the sky
hear our solemn litany.

By thine hour of dire despair;
by thine agony in prayer;
by the Cross, the nail, the thorn,
piercing spear, and torturing scorn;
by the gloom that veiled the skies
o'er the dreadful Sacrifice:
listen to our humble cry,
hear our solemn litany.

By thy deep expiring groan;
by the sad se-pul-chral stone;
by the vault whose dark abode
held in vain the rising God:
O, from earth to heaven restored,
mighty, re-ascended Lord,
listen, listen to the cry
of our solemn litany.

[Sir R. Grant (1785-1838)]

(When the office of Compline is not prayed, the Commendation Prayer and the Canticle of Simeon (see pages 10-11) are included here.)

GOING FORTH
May the God of peace
make you holy in every way
and keep your whole being—
spirit, soul, and body—
free from every fault
at the coming of our Lord Jesus Christ.

(1 Thessalonians 5:23)

Let us bless the Lord.
Thanks be to God! Amen.

Morning Prayer

For Thursdays in Lent

CALL TO PRAYER
  O Lord, open my lips
  and my mouth shall proclaim your praise.
  Repent and turn from your transgressions.
  Get yourselves a new heart and new spirit.
  Why will you die?
  I have no pleasure in the death of anyone, says the Lord God.
  Turn, then, and live!

(Ezekiel 18:30-32 sel.)

HYMN [66.66; Tune: DOLOMITE CHANT, *UMH* 455]

I hunger and I thirst;
Jesus, my manna be;
Ye living water, burst
Out of the rock for me.

Thou bruised and broken Bread,
My life-long wants supply;
As living souls are fed,
O feed me, or I die.

Thou true life-giving Vine,
Let me thy sweetness prove;
Renew my life with thine,
Refresh my soul with love.

Rough paths my feet have trod
Since first their course began;
Feed me, thou Bread of God;
Help me, thou Son of Man.

For still the desert lies
My thirsting soul before;
O living waters, rise
Within me evermore.

[JOHN SAMUEL BEWLEY MONSELL, 1811-75]

MORNING PRAYER
  Almighty God, who sees that we have no power of ourselves to help
  ourselves; keep us this day both outwardly in our bodies, and inwardly
  in our souls; that we may be defended from all adversities which may
  happen to the body, and from all evil thoughts which may assault and
  hurt the soul; through Jesus Christ our Lord. **Amen.**

[GREGORIAN SACRAMENTARY]

PSALTER   Psalm 130
> From the depths I <u>call</u> to *you,*
> Lord, <u>hear</u> my *cry.*
> Catch the sound <u>of</u> my *voice*
> raised <u>up -</u> , *pleading.*
>
> If you record our sins,
>   Lord, who <u>could</u> sur-*vive?*
> But because you forgive
>   we <u>stand</u> in *awe.*
> I trust in God's word,
>   I trust <u>in</u> the *Lord.*
> More than sentries for dawn
>   I watch <u>for</u> the *Lord.*
>
> More than <u>sentries</u> for *dawn*
> let <u>Is</u>-rael *watch.*
> The Lord will bring mercy
>   and <u>grant</u> full *pardon.*
> The Lord will free Israel
>   from <u>all</u> its *sins.*

THE GLORIA   (*see back cover*)

SCRIPTURE   (*see daily lectionary*)

—*silent reflection*—

CANTICLE OF ZECHARIAH   (*see back cover*)

[READINGS(S) FOR MEDITATION AND REFLECTION

PRAYERS
> PRAYERS OF INTERCESSION AND SUPPLICATION
> O God our healer and our health,
> we bring our brokenness to you.
> Mend what is twisted and paralyzed in us . . .
> Lay your hands upon your Church
>   where it is blind and deaf and without voice . . .
> Bend down and write in the dirt before an accused
>   and disobedient world . . .
> See with mercy all whose needs and conditions
>   we lift before you now . . .   [DTB]

—*silent prayer*—

[OTHER SELECTED PRAYERS   (*see pages 17ff*)

[PRAYERS OF SPECIAL INTENTION (*such as the following*)
 [INTERCESSIONS FOR THE ORDER OF SAINT LUKE (*see back cover*)
 [A COLLECT FOR THE ORDER OF SAINT LUKE (*see p. 248*)

CONCLUDING PRAYER
Great God, whose Son Jesus came among us to serve: Teach us the meaning of servanthood. Grant that we may know when to act and when to show restraint, when to speak and when to remain silent, so that we may serve you faithfully and fulfill your purpose for us; through our Servant Christ. **Amen.**

[GLH]

THE LORD'S PRAYER (*see p. 248*)
 (*SEE UMH 270-271 FOR MUSICAL SETTINGS*)

HYMN [78.78.88; Tune: LIEBSTER JESU, *UMH* 596]
Blessed Jesus, at thy word
we are gathered all to hear thee;
let our hearts and souls be stirred
now to seek and love and fear thee;
by thy teachings sweet and holy,
drawn from earth to love thee solely.

All our knowledge, sense, and sight
lie in deepest darkness shrouded,
till thy spirit breaks our night
with the beams of truth unclouded.
Thou alone to God canst win us;
Thou must work all good within us.

Glorious Lord, thyself impart!
Light of light, from God proceeding,
open thou our ears and heart;
help us by thy spirit's pleading;
hear the cry thy people raises;
hear, and bless our prayers and praises.

[TOBIAS CLAUSNITZER, 1663, TRANS. BY CATHERINE WINKWORTH, 1858]

GOING FORTH
The Lord Jesus Christ be near you to defend you, within you to re-fresh you, around you to preserve you, before you to guide you, behind you to justify you, above you to bless you; who lives and reigns with the Almighty, and with the Holy Spirit, one God for evermore.

[10TH C. PRAYER, ALT TAR]

Let us bless the Lord.
 Thanks be to God! Amen.

Evening Prayer
For Thursdays in Lent

ENTRANCE OF THE LIGHT
> O God, come to our assistance.
> **O Lord, hasten to help us.**
> O Israel, hope in God
> with whom there is steadfast love
> and plenteous redemption.

(Psalm 130:7)

HYMN OF LIGHT (*The "Phos hilaron;" see front cover*)

[EVENING PRAYER CANTICLE (*see front cover*)

CONFESSION AND PARDON
> O Son of God, who walks among the seven golden lampstands: the night of sin has covered us. We have passed our lives in darkness and have returned to our old selves: hard of heart, anxious in spirit, double minded in thought and action. So composed we have sinned against you and our neighbor.

—silence for examination of conscience—

[*see UMH 482-484 for musical settings of the* Kyrie]
> *Kyrie eleison.*
> *Christe eleison.*
> *Kyrie eleison.*

—silence—

> Forgive us and heal us. Restore us to our right minds and our first love. **Amen.**

[DTB]

> In Christ, we are a forgiven people.
> **Thanks be to God.**

PSALTER Psalm 91
I

> All you sheltered by the Most High,
> who live in Al-<u>mighty</u> God's *shadow*,
> say to the Lord, "My refuge, my fortress,
> my God in <u>whom</u> I *trust!*"

God will free you from hunters' snares,
  will save you from <u>dead</u>-ly *plague*,
will cover you like a nesting bird.
  God's <u>wings</u> will *shelter you.*

No nighttime terror <u>shall</u> you *fear,*
no arrows <u>shot</u> by *day,*
no plague that <u>prowls</u> the *dark,*
no wasting <u>scourge</u> at *noon.*

A thousand may fall at your side,
  ten thousand at <u>your</u> right *hand.*
But you shall live unharmed:
  God is <u>stur</u>-dy *armor.*

You have only to open your eyes
  to see how the wicked <u>are</u> re-*paid.*
You have the Lord as refuge,
  have made the Most <u>High</u> your *stronghold.*

No evil shall ever touch you,
  no harm come <u>near</u> your *home.*
God instructs angels
  to guard you where-<u>ever</u> you *go.*
With their hands they support you,
  so your foot will not <u>strike</u> a *stone.*
You will tread on lion and viper,
  trample tawny <u>lion</u> and *dragon.*

"I deliver all who cling to me,
  raise the ones who <u>know</u> my *name,*
answer those who call me,
  stand with <u>those</u> in *trouble.*
These I rescue and honor,
  satisfy <u>with</u> long *life,*
and show my <u>power</u> to *save."*

THE GLORIA (*see back cover*)

SCRIPTURE (*see daily lectionary*)

                  —*silent reflection*—

CANTICLE OF MARY (*see front cover*)

[READING(S) FOR MEDITATION AND REFLECTION

PRAYERS

PRAYERS OF THANKSGIVING AND INTERCESSION
God of Israel descending into Egypt to face oppression and death,
    bring us out of Egypt in these Lenten days
    and renew your promises to us.
With the catechumens who will come through the baptismal waters,
    renew your covenant with us.
Prepare our souls and bodies to rejoice in your salvation,
    even as you prepare us by acts of repentance and works of mercy.
Deal gently with the brash and invincible
    who risk destruction.
Refresh all who are cast down.
In all people, fix your love for the poor and suffering.
Bless the new born and the twice born.
Call your church to rest with you in this night's Bethany.
From the meager scraps of bread and fish available,
    feed the hungry and satisfy the hungry hearts with love's plenty.
In the silence of day's end, invite us to yield ourselves
    to your transforming presence . . .

[DTB]

(*here observe a time of intention to let the Holy Spirit work in you beyond
thoughts, words, or emotions*)

—silent prayer—

[OTHER SELECTED PRAYERS (*see pages 4ff*)

[PRAYERS OF SPECIAL INTENTION (*such as the following*)
    [INTERCESSIONS FOR THE ORDER OF SAINT LUKE (*see back cover*)
    [A COLLECT FOR THE ORDER OF SAINT LUKE (*see p. 248*)

CONCLUDING PRAYER
Merciful God, you are just in your judgments but rich in kindness:
grant us strength of resolve and an openness to overcome our weak-
nesses. We ask this through Christ our Savior. **Amen.**

[PWC]

THE LORD'S PRAYER (*see p. 248*)
    (*See UMH 270-271 for musical settings*)

HYMN: [LM; Tune: TALLIS CANON, *UMH* 682]

O thou to whose all-searching sight
The darkness shineth as the light,
Search, prove my heart; it longs for thee;
O burst these bonds, and set it free!

Wash out its stains, refine its dross,
Nail my affections to the cross;
Hallow each thought; let all within
Be clean, as thou, my Lord, art clean.

If in this darksome wild I stray,
Be thou my light, be thou my way;
No foes, no evils need I fear,
No harm, while, thou, my God, art near.

Savior, whate'er thy steps I see,
Dauntless, untired, I follow thee.
O let thy hand support me still,
And lead me to thy holy hill!

[NICOLAUS L. VON ZINZENDORF 1700-1760; TR. JOHN WESLEY]

(When the office of Compline is not prayed, the Commendation Prayer and the Canticle of Simeon (see pages 10-11) are included here.)

GOING FORTH

May the Cross of the Son of God who is mightier than all the hosts of Satan, and more glorious than all the angels of heaven, abide with us in our going out and our coming in! By day and night, at morning and at evening, at all times and in all places may it protect and defend us! From the wrath of evil people, from the assaults of evil spirits, from the foes invisible, from the snares of the devil, from all passions that beguile the soul and body, may it guard, protect, and deliver us.

[ADAPTED FROM THE CHRISTARAKANA, BCP, CHURCH OF INDIA, PAKISTAN, BURMA, AND CEYLON.]

Let us bless the Lord.
Thanks be to God. Amen.

Morning Prayer
For Fridays in Lent

CALL TO PRAYER
> O Lord, open my lips
> **and my mouth shall proclaim your praise.**
> May those who sow with tears
> reap with songs of joy.
>
> (Psalm 126:6; adapted from BCP Psalter)

HYMN [LM; Tune: DEO GRACIAS, *UMH* 267]

O love, how deep, how broad, how high,
it fills the heart with ecstasy,
that God, the Son of God, should take
our mortal form for mortals' sake!

For us baptized, for us he bore
his holy fast and hungered sore,
for us temptation sharp he knew;
for us the tempter overthrew.

For us he prayed; for us he taught;
for us his daily works he wrought;
by words and signs and actions thus
still seeking not himself, but us.

For us to evil power betrayed,
scourged, mocked, in purple robe arrayed,
he bore the shameful cross and death,
for us gave up his dying breath.

For us he rose from death again;
for us he went on high to reign;
for us he sent his Spirit here,
to guide, to strengthen, and to cheer.

All glory to our Lord and God
for love so deep, so high, so broad:
the Trinity whom we adore,
forever and forevermore.

[BENJAMIN WEBB, 1854; ALT]

MORNING PRAYER
> God who reaches out to us: You have called us to be your people.
> May we have the strength to acknowledge our failure to live in your
> freedom. Help us to know throughout this day that when we turn to
> you, you are already coming with joy to welcome us; through Jesus
> Christ our brother. **Amen.**
>
> [GLH]

PSALTER: Psalm 6 (spoken)

Stop rebuking me, Lord,
  hold back your rage.
Have pity, for I am spent;
  heal me, hurt to the bone,
  wracked to the limit.
Lord, how long? How long?

Repent, Lord, save me.
You promised; keep faith!
In death, who remembers you?
In Sheol, who gives you thanks?

Night after night I lie exhausted,
  hollow-eyed with grief,
  my pillow soaked with tears:
  all because of my foes.

Get away from me, scoundrels!
The Lord has heard my tears.
God hears my pleading
  and will answer my prayer.
My foes will be shamed, shocked,
  turned back in sudden panic.

THE GLORIA (*see back cover*)

SCRIPTURE (*see daily lectionary*)

—silent reflection—

CANTICLE OF ZECHARIAH (*see back cover*)

[READING(S) FOR MEDITATION AND REFLECTION

PRAYERS

PRAYERS OF THANKSGIVING AND SUPPLICATION
We bless and praise and magnify you, O God of mercy. You have led
us out of the shadows of night once more into the light of day. To
your loving-kindness we make our entreaty: be merciful to us in our
misdeeds; accept our prayers in the fullness of your compassion, for
you are our refuge from one generation to another.

We await the Day of justice and reconciliation when all enter the gates of the new Jerusalem and feast at your heavenly banquet. Until that day, cause us to discern that many have not yet entered your banquet hall. Instead of lapsing into bad manners by beginning to feast while you are still looking for the missing guests, prompt us to prayerful search for the countless millions in the world who languish in suffering, injustice, hunger, war, isolation and abuse.

With eyes and hearts open to the empty places at the table, we pray:
for youth who long for life . . .
for refugees and exiles . . .
for all who suffer and are in trouble . . .
for leaders who have power for good and evil . . .
for the Church sleeping in the light . . .
for those people and concerns that arise in the silence now . . .

[ADAPTED FROM A GREEK PRAYER; DTB]

—silent prayer—

[OTHER SELECTED PRAYERS (*see pages 16ff*)

[PRAYERS OF SPECIAL INTENTION (*such as the following*)
  [INTERCESSIONS FOR THE ORDER OF SAINT LUKE (*see back cover*)
  [A COLLECT FOR THE ORDER OF SAINT LUKE (*see p. 248*)

CONCLUDING PRAYER
Suffer the true Sun of your Righteousness to shine in our hearts; enlighten our reason, and purify our senses, that we may walk honestly as in the day, in the way of your commandments, and reach at last the life eternal, where we shall rejoice in your Life, and in your Light shall we see light. **Amen.**

[DTB]

THE LORD'S PRAYER (*see p. 248*)
  (*See UMH 270-271 for musical settings*)

HYMN [LM; Tune: CONDITOR ALME; *UMH* 692]
O Sun of Righteousness, we pray
our darkened minds may know thy day,
that healing light may shine once more
as day to earth Thou dost restore.

While praying in this time apart,
oh, grant us, now a contrite heart
and may by kindness those be turned
who long Thy patient love have spurned.

That day draws nigh, Thy saving hour
when all things made anew shall flow'r;
oh, let us greet with joyful face
that day which brings us back Thy grace.

May all creation worship Thee,
oh blessed, holy Trinity,
and we, by mercy now restored,
may sing a new song to the Lord.

[ADAPTED FROM A TRADITIONAL DAILY OFFICE HYMN, DTB, DWV]

GOING FORTH
May the eternal God bless and keep us, guard our bodies, save our souls, direct our thoughts, and bring us safe to our eternal home, where the ever blessed Trinity lives and reigns, one God for ever and ever.

[SARUM BREVIARY ALT]

Let us bless the Lord.
Thanks be to God! Amen.

Evening Prayer
For Fridays in Lent

ENTRANCE OF THE LIGHT
O God, come to our assistance.
O Lord, hasten to help us.
As Moses lifted up the serpent in the wilderness,
so must the Son of Man be lifted up,
that whoever believes in him may have eternal life.

(John 3:14-15)

HYMN OF LIGHT (*The "Phos hilaron;" see cover 2*)

[EVENING PRAYER CANTICLE (*see cover 2*)

CONFESSION AND PARDON
O God, whose nature and property is ever to have mercy and to forgive, receive our humble petitions. Though we be tied and bound with the chain of our sins, yet may the pity of your great mercy loose us.

—silence—

O Lord Jesus Christ, who gave your life for us that we might receive pardon and peace; mercifully cleanse us from all sin, and evermore keep us in your favor and love, who lives and reigns with the Almighty and the Holy Spirit, ever one God, world without end. Amen..

[ADAPTED FROM 6TH C. PRAYERS OF GREGORY THE GREAT AND AN ANCIENT COLLECT; TAR)]

In Jesus Christ, we are forgiven.
Thanks be to God!

PSALTER   Psalm 115
Not to us, Lord, not to us,
  but to your <u>name</u> give *glory,*
because of your love,
  because <u>of</u> your *truth.*
Why do the nations say,
  "Where <u>is</u> their *God?"*
Our God is in the heavens
  and <u>answers</u> to *no one.*

Their gods are crafted by hand,
  mere <u>silver</u> and *gold,*
with mouths that are mute
  and eyes that are blind,
  with ears that are deaf
  and noses that <u>can</u>-not *smell.*
Their hands cannot feel,
  their feet cannot walk,
  their <u>throats</u> are *silent.*
Their makers, their worshipers
  will <u>be</u> just *like them.*

Let Israel trust God,
  their <u>help</u> and *shield.*
Let the house of Aaron trust God,
  their <u>help</u> and *shield.*
Let all be-<u>lievers</u> trust *God,*
  their <u>help</u> and *shield.*

The Lord has remembered us
  and will bless us,
  will bless the house of Israel,
  will bless the <u>house</u> of *Aaron.*
God will bless all believers,
  the small <u>and</u> the *great.*
May God bless you more and more,
  bless <u>all</u> your *children.*
May you truly be blest
  by the maker of <u>heaven</u> and *earth.*

To the Lord belong the heavens,
   to us the <u>earth</u> be-*low!*
The dead sing no Hallelujah,
   nor do those in the <u>si</u>-lent *ground.*
But we will bless you, Lord,
   now <u>and</u> for *ever.*
Hal-<u>le</u> - *lujah!*

THE GLORIA (*see back cover*)

SCRIPTURE (*see daily lectionary*)

—*silent reflection*—

CANTICLE OF MARY (*see front cover*)

[READING(S) FOR MEDITATION AND REFLECTION

PRAYERS

PRAYERS OF SUPPLICATION AND INTERCESSION
Senõr, at the end of this day's toil and struggle
   we bless you for your sustaining and sanctifying grace.
May every wound be accompanied by consolation.
May every step backward be made into a dance of grace.
In every routine act and drudgery may we now see the way of the
cross in company with Jesus.
Steadfast savior,
   mend the broken hearts of the divorcing, the abandoned
      and the grieving . . .
   pray yourself in the searching, the powerful
      and the angry among us . . .
   lead your church to courageous witness in every nation
      and place of service . . .
   grant peace to the worried, restless and violent . . .
   stay our minds upon the mystery of your presence in the silence . . .
                                                                        [DTB]

   (here simply rest in the presence of God for an extended time.)

—*silent prayer*—

[OTHER SELECTED PRAYERS (*see pages 4ff*)

[PRAYERS OF SPECIAL INTENTION (*such as the following*)
   [INTERCESSIONS FOR THE ORDER OF SAINT LUKE (*see back cover*)
   [A COLLECT FOR THE ORDER OF SAINT LUKE (*see p. 248*)

CONCLUDING PRAYER
We pray to you, uncreated and eternal God.
Hold out your hand to us and help us to our feet.
Merciful God, pull us upward.
Give us the courage to stand up without shame or guilt.
Revoke the death sentence against us
and write our names in the book of life
with all your holy prophets and apostles. **Amen.**

[SERAPION OF THUMIS, FOURTH CENTURY]

THE LORD'S PRAYER *(see p. 248)*
(See UMH 270-271 for musical settings)

HYMN [6666; Tune: LENOX (without refrain), *UMH* 379]
My spirit longs for thee
within my troubled breast,
though I unworthy be
of so divine a guest.

Of so divine a guest
unworthy though I be,
yet has my heart no rest
unless it comes from thee.

Unless it come from thee,
in vain I look around;
in all that I can see
no rest is to be found.

No rest is to be found
but in thy bless-ed love:
O let my wish be crowned,
and send it from above.

[J. BYROM, 1691-1763]

(When the office of Compline is not prayed, the Commendation Prayer and the Canticle of Simeon (see pages 10-11) are included here.)

GOING FORTH
The God of peace, who brought again from the dead our Lord Jesus, that great shepherd of sheep, through the blood of the everlasting covenant, make us perfect in every good work to do God's will, working in us that which is well-pleasing in God's sight; through Jesus Christ, to whom be glory for ever and ever.

(Adapted from Hebrews 13: 20, 21)

Let us bless the Lord.
Thanks be to God!

Morning Prayer

CALL TO PRAISE AND PRAYER

O Lord, open my lips
and my mouth shall proclaim your praise.
But store up for yourselves treasures in heaven, where neither moth
nor rust consumes and where thieves do not break in and steal. For
where your treasure is, there your heart will be also.

(Matthew 6:20-21)

HYMN [LM; Tune: MARYTON *UMH* 430]

Ho! Everyone that thirsts, draw nigh,
come to the living waters, come!
Mercy and free salvation buy;
return ye weary wanderers, home.

See from the rock a fountain rise!
For you in healing streams it rolls,
money you need not bring, nor price,
o laboring, burdened, sin-sick souls.

Why seek ye that which is not bread,
nor can your hungry souls sustain?
On ashes, husks, and air you feed;
and spend your little all in vain.

I bid you all my goodness prove;
my promises for all are free;
Come, taste the manna of my love,
and let your soul delight in me.

[CHARLES WESLEY (1707-1788)]

MORNING PRAYER

O God of Light, Creator of Life, Giver of Wisdom, Benefactor of our
souls, giving to the fainthearted who put their trust in you those things
into which the angels desire to look; O Sovereign, who has brought
us up from the depths of darkness to light, who has given us life from
death, who has graciously bestowed upon us freedom from slavery,
and who has scattered the darkness of sin within us; also enlighten
the eyes of our understanding this day, and sanctify us wholly in soul,
body, and spirit. **Amen.**

[ADAPTED FROM THE LITURGY OF ST. MARK, 3RD C.; TAR]

I

The sky tells the <u>glory</u> of *God,*
tells the genius <u>of</u> God's *work.*
Day carries the <u>news</u> to *day,*
night brings the <u>message</u> to *night,*

without a word, with - <u>out</u> a *sound,*
without a <u>voice</u> being *heard,*
yet their message <u>fills</u> the *world,*
their news <u>reaches</u> its *rim.*

There God has <u>pitched</u> a *tent*
for the sun to rest and <u>rise</u> re-*newed*
like a bridegroom <u>rising</u> from *bed,*
an athlete eager to <u>run</u> the *race.*

It springs from the <u>edge</u> of the *earth,*
runs a course a-<u>cross</u> the *sky*
to win the race at <u>hea</u>-ven's *end.*
Nothing on earth es-<u>capes</u> its *heat.*

II

God's perfect law re-<u>vives</u> the *soul.*
God's stable rule <u>guides</u> the *simple.*
God's just demands de-<u>light</u> the *heart.*
God's clear commands <u>sharp</u>-en *vision.*

God's faultless decrees <u>stand</u> for *ever.*
God's right judgments <u>keep</u> their *truth.*
Their worth is more than gold, the <u>pur</u>-est *gold;*
their taste richer than honey, <u>sweet</u> from the *comb.*

Keeping them <u>makes</u> me *rich,*
they <u>bring</u> me *light;*
yet faults <u>hide</u> with-*in us,*
for-<u>give</u> me *mine.*

Keep my pride in check,
   <u>break</u> its *grip;*
I shall be free of blame
   for <u>dead</u>-ly *sin.*
Keep me, thought and word,
   in <u>your</u> good *grace.*
Lord, you are my savior,
   you <u>are</u> my *rock.*

THE GLORIA (*see back cover*)

SCRIPTURE (*see daily lectionary*)

—*silent reflection*—

CANTICLE OF ZECHARIAH (*see back cover*)

[READING(S) FOR MEDITATION AND REFLECTION

PRAYERS

PRAYERS OF THANKSGIVING AND SUPPLICATION
Eternal God, whose Son Jesus Christ endured hunger that our souls might be fed, and knew thirst that our hearts might be watered, have mercy on us. We thanklessly accept his love, ignoring the pain it cost him; we refuse to rejoice in his life, death, and resurrection, his living presence, the forgiveness of our sins, and his glorious promises to us of all that is to come. In this Lent, alert our souls to his loving presence; clear our eyes, and open our ears, that we may see him suffering for us, hear him calling us by name, and know that he longs to be with us always; it is in his name that we pray. **Amen.**

—*silent prayer*—

[OTHER SELECTED PRAYERS (*see pages 16ff*)

[PRAYERS OF SPECIAL INTENTION (*such as the following*)
    [INTERCESSIONS FOR THE ORDER OF SAINT LUKE (*see back cover*)
    [A COLLECT FOR THE ORDER OF SAINT LUKE (*see p. 248*)

CONCLUDING PRAYER
O God, who is the unsearchable abyss of peace, the ineffable sea of love, the fountain of blessings, and the bestower of affection: open to us today the sea of your love, and water us with the plenteous streams from the riches of your grace. Enkindle in us the fire of your love; sow in us your fear; strengthen our weakness by your power; bind us closely to you and to each other in one firm bond of unity; for the sake of Jesus Christ. **Amen.**

[ADAPTED FROM SYRIAN CLEMENTINE LITURGY, 1ST C.; TAR]

THE LORD'S PRAYER (*see p. 248*)
    (*See* UMH 270-271 *for musical settings*)

HYMN [SM; Tune: ST. MICHAEL, *UMH* 372]

Make me a captive, Lord,
and then I shall be free.
Force me to render up my sword,
and I shall conqueror be.
I sink in life's alarms
when by myself I stand;
imprison me within thine arms,
and strong shall be my hand.

My heart is weak and poor
until it master find;
it has no spring of action sure,
it varies with the wind.
It cannot freely move til thou has wrought its chain;
enslave it with thy matchless love,
and deathless it shall reign.

My power is faint and low
til I have learned to serve;
it lacks the needed fire to glow,
It lacks the breeze to nerve.
It cannot drive the world
until itself be driven;
its flag can only be unfurled
when thou shalt breathe from heaven.

My will is not my own
til thou hast made it thine;
if it would reach a monarch's throne,
it must its crown resign.
It only stands unbent
amid the clashing strife,
when on thy bosom it has leant,
and found in thee its life.

[GEORGE MATHESON, 1890]

GOING FORTH

May the Lord bless us with all good and keep us from all evil; may
God give light to our hearts with loving wisdom, and be gracious to
us with eternal knowledge; may God's loving countenance be lifted
upon us for eternal peace.

[ADAPTED FROM DEAD SEA SCROLLS; TAR]

Let us bless the Lord.
Thanks be to God.

Vígíl
for Saturday Evenings in Lent
(replacing Evening Prayer and Compline)

ENTRANCE OF THE LIGHT
> Light and peace in Jesus Christ.
> **Thanks be to God**
> Send out your light and your truth;
> let them lead us.

(Psalm 43:3)

HYMN OF LIGHT (*The "Phos hilaron," see cover 2*)

THANKSGIVING FOR THE LIGHT
> Thanks be to you, O Lord,
> the Light, the Way, the Truth, the Life;
> in you there is no darkness, or death.
>
> You are the Light without which there is darkness;
> the Way without which there is wandering;
> the Truth without which there is error;
> the life without which there is Death.
>
> Lord, say: "let there be Light,"
> and I shall see Light, and disdain Darkness;
> I shall see the Way and avoid wandering;
> I shall see the Truth and shun error;
> I shall see Life and escape Death.
>
> Illuminate, O illuminate my soul
> which sits in darkness and the shadow of Death;
> and direct my feet into the way of peace. **Amen.**

[AUGUSTINE, 4TH C. ALT]

[EVENING PRAYER CANTICLE (selected from Psalm 141)
A CHANT FORM: (*see cover 2*)
(*See UMH, bottom of p. 850 for a musical setting of the antiphon by Arlo Duba*)

B METRICAL FORM:
[8888.88; Tune: ST. PETERSBURG *UMH* 153]
> Come quickly, Lord, I call on you;
> And hear my voice, my cry for help.
> Control my lips and tongue, O Lord,
> And save my heart from evil's grasp
> Let my prayer rise like incense, Lord,
> My hands, an ev'ning sacrifice.

Help me accept rebuke as grace,
And guard me from all bitterness.
All wicked ways may I resist
And never share in sensuous feasts.
Let my prayer rise like incense, Lord,
My hands, an ev'ning sacrifice.

Protect me from the Evil One,
And rule my life through Christ your Son,
With Holy Fire my sins consume,
And flood my soul with love divine,
My heart shall rise as incense, Lord,
My life, your living sacrifice.

[SF]

CONFESSION AND PARDON

O Lamb of God, we have forgotten our baptismal profession
in our daily life:
  we have embraced incompatible loyalties,
  we have not linked baptism with martyrdom.
  we have let theology and liturgy be diversions
    rather than calls to faithfulness.
O Christ, renew the love and courage we had at first. Bring us down
from the towers of speculation and out from caves of inwardness to
loyalty in the world where your passion still calls us to resist evil and
share in your victory of love. Jesus, forgive our sin and heal our will.

[DTB]

—silence for examination of conscience—

"He saved us, not because of any works of righteousness that we had
done, but according to his mercy through the water of rebirth and
renewal of the Holy Spirit."

(Titus 3:5)

In the name of Jesus Christ we are forgiven and called.
  Thanks be to God!

THE BLESSING

Lord, grant us your blessing.
Let us pray:
Kindle in our hearts, O God,
  the flame of that love which never ceases,
  that it may burn in us, giving light to others.
May we shine for ever in your temple,
  set on fire with your eternal light,
  even your Son Jesus Christ,
  our Saviour and our Redeemer. **Amen.**

[St. Columba, CCP]

FIRST READING (*from the Sunday Lectionary or Daily Lectionary*)

PSALTER Psalm 43
  Decide in my favor, God,
   plead my case a-<u>gainst</u> the *hateful,*
  defend me from liars and thugs.
   For you are <u>God</u> my *fortress.*
  Why have you for-<u>got</u>-ten *me?*
  Why am I bent double
   under the <u>weight</u> of *enemies?*

  Send your <u>light</u> and *truth.*
  They will escort me
   to the holy mountain
   where you <u>make</u> your *home.*
  I will approach the altar of God,
   God, my <u>high</u>-est *joy,*
  and praise you with the harp,
   <u>God</u>, my *God.*

  Why are you <u>sad</u>, my *heart?*
  Why <u>do</u> you *grieve?*
  Wait <u>for</u> the *Lord.*
  I will yet praise <u>God</u> my *savior.*

THE GLORIA (*see back cover; musical setting, UMH 72; or:*)
 Glory to God, Love abounding be-<u>fore</u> all *ages;*
 Glory to God, Love shown forth in the self-emptying of <u>Je</u>-sus *Christ;*
 Glory to god, Love poured out through the <u>gift</u> of the *Spirit,*
  Who fashions and renews the <u>face</u> of the *earth;*
 Glory to the holy and <u>bless</u>-ed *Trinity!*
 All things abiding in Love,
  Love abiding <u>in</u> all *things,*
 As it is now, <u>ev</u>-er *was,*
  And ever shall be for endless ages. <u>A</u>-*men.*

                   [DNP]

EPISTLE READING (*from the Sunday Lectionary or Daily Lectionary*)

READING OF THE GOSPEL
 (*from the Sunday Lectionary or Daily Lectionary*)

CANTICLE OF REDEMPTION (*De Profundis*)
 [Psalm Tone Five (for a metrical form, see *UMH* 515)]
  Out of the depths I cry to you, O God;
   Lord, <u>hear</u> my *voice.*
  Incline your ear to the voice of my <u>sup</u>-pli-*cation.*

If you were to mark all iniquities,
   O God, <u>who</u> could *stand?*
But there is forgiveness with you
   that you <u>may</u> be *worshiped.*

I wait for the Lord, <u>my</u> soul *waits,*
and in God's <u>word</u> I *hope;*
My soul waits for the Lord
   more than those who watch <u>for</u> the *morning;*
more than those who watch <u>for</u> the *morning.*

O Israel, trust the *Lord;*
   with God there is mercy and plen-<u>teous</u> re-*demption*
for the *Lord*
   will redeem Israel from <u>all</u> in-*iquities.*

(Psalm 130; alt DWV)

—silent reflection—

[READING(S) FOR MEDITATION AND REFLECTION

PRAYERS
   PRAYERS OF SUPPLICATION AND INTERCESSION
   In peace, we pray to you, Lord God:
      For all people in their daily life and work . . .
      For our families, friends, and for those who are alone . . .
      For this community, the nation, and the world . . .
      For all who work for justice, freedom and peace . . .
      For the just and proper use of your creation . . .
      For the victims of hunger, fear, injustice, and oppression . . .
      For all who are in danger, sorrow, or any kind of trouble . . .
      For those who minister to the sick, the friendless, and the needy . . .
      For the peace and unity of the Church of God . . .
      For all who proclaim the Gospel,
         and all who seek the truth . . .

Lord, let your loving-kindness be upon us
   for we put our trust in you.

[BCP, FORM VI]

—silent prayer—

[OTHER SELECTED PRAYERS *(see pages 4ff)*

[PRAYERS OF SPECIAL INTENTION *(such as the following)*

[INTERCESSIONS FOR THE ORDER OF SAINT LUKE (*see back cover*)
[A COLLECT FOR THE ORDER OF SAINT LUKE (*see p. 248*)

CONCLUDING PRAYER
Accept the evening thanksgiving of your baptized people, O Fountain of all good. You have led us safely through the length of the day; you daily bless us with many mercies. Give us the hope of resurrection to eternal life; through Jesus Christ our Lord. **Amen.**

[ADAPTED FROM 5TH C. COLLECT; TAR]

THE LORD'S PRAYER (*see p. 248*)
(*See* UMH 270-271 *for musical settings*)

HYMN [LM; TUNE: HURSLEY, *UMH* 616)]

Creator of the world, give ear,
with gracious love our prayers to hear,
prayers which our longing spirits raise
who keep this Lent of forty days.

Each heart is open unto thee;
thou knowest our infirmities.
Now we repent, give us thy grace,
that we may each thy love embrace.

Spare us, O God; we now confess
our sins and seek your holiness
that for the glory of thy Name,
our sin-sick souls may health regain.

Grant, blessed, holy Trinity,
One God, eternal Unity;
that baptized by thy grace and blessed
we may bear fruit of holiness.

[AUDI, BENIGNE CONDITOR; ATR TO GREGORY THE GREAT, 540-604, DWV]

COMMENDATION
In peace we will lie down and sleep.
In the Lord alone we safely rest.
Guide us waking, O Lord, and guard us sleeping,
That awake we may watch with Christ,
And asleep we may rest in peace.

May the divine help remain with us always.
And with those who are absent from us.

—silence—

Into your hands, O Lord, I commend my spirit,
For you have redeemed me, O Lord,
O God of Truth.

[SARUM BREVIARY, PS. 4:8 AND 30:5, ADAPTED]

CANTICLE OF SIMEON (*The Nunc Dimittis;* Luke 2::29-32)
(*See* UMH 225-226 *for metrical versions*)
Lord, you have now set your <u>ser</u>-vant free
to go in peace as <u>you</u> have *promised;*
for these eyes of mine have <u>seen</u> the Savior,
Whom you have prepared for all the <u>world</u> to *see.*
A Light to en-<u>lighten</u> the *nations,*
And the glory of your <u>peo</u>-ple *Israel.*

[ICET]

GOING FORTH
May God bless us with all heavenly benediction, and make us pure and holy by divine perception. May the riches of God's glory abound in us. May God instruct us with the word of truth, inform us with the Gospel of salvation, and enrich us with love, through Jesus Christ, our Lord.

[ADAPTED FROM GELESIAN SACRAMENTARY; TAR]

Let us bless the Lord.
Thanks be to God.

Morning Prayer
For Sundays in Lent

CALL TO PRAISE AND PRAYER

O Lord, open my lips
and my mouth shall proclaim your praise.
All I want is to know is Christ and the power of his resurrection and
the sharing of his sufferings by becoming like him in his death.

(Philippians 3:10)

CANTICLE OF PRAISE TO GOD: *The Venite Exultemus*
[Ps. 951-7; 96:8b, 9, 13b]   (*For a four-part musical version, see* UMH 91)

Come, sing with <u>joy</u> to *God*,
shout to our <u>savior,</u> our *rock*.
Enter God's <u>presence</u> with *praise*,
enter with <u>shouting</u> and *song*.

A great God is the Lord, over the <u>gods</u> like a *king*.
God cradles the depths of the earth, holds fast the <u>moun</u>-tain *peaks*.
God shaped the <u>ocean</u> and *owns it*,
formed the <u>earth</u> *by hand*.

Come, bow <u>down</u> and *worship*,
kneel to the <u>Lord</u> our *maker*.
This is our <u>God</u>, our *shepherd*,
we are the flock <u>led</u> with *care*.

Bring gifts to the temple, bow down, <u>all</u> the *earth*,
tremble in God's <u>ho</u>-ly *presence*.
[The Lord] comes to <u>judge</u> the *nations*,
to set the earth aright, restoring the <u>world</u> to *order*.

[ICEL]

MORNING PRAYER

O God, you renew us by our celebration of the resurrection of your
Son: grant us fresh strength to meet the challenges of this new week,
that we may come to you faithfully now and always. Amen.

[PWC]

PSALTER Psalm 28

I

I call out, <u>Lord</u> my *rock*.
Do <u>not</u> be *deaf*,
do <u>not</u> keep *silent*.
Without you <u>I</u> must *die*.

Hear my cry for mercy,
   my <u>call</u> for *help;*
I stretch out my hands
   toward your <u>ho</u>-ly *temple.*
Do not drag me <u>off</u> like the *wicked*
who speak peace to friends
   but have malice <u>in</u> their *hearts.*

Pay them in <u>their</u> own *coin.*
What they do is evil;
   give them <u>what</u> they de-*serve.*
The ways of the Lord
   mean <u>nothing</u> to *them.*
May God destroy their world
   and <u>never</u> re-*build it!*

II

Blessed be the Lord
   who <u>hears</u> my *cry.*
God is the strong shield
   in <u>whom my</u> heart *trusts.*
When help comes to me,
   joy <u>fills</u> my *heart*
and I thank <u>God</u> in *song.*

Strength comes <u>from</u> the *Lord,*
salvation for <u>his</u> a-*nointed.*
Save your <u>cho</u>-sen *people.*
Bless and shepherd them
   and <u>keep them</u> for *ever.*

THE GLORIA (*see back cover*)

SCRIPTURE   (*see daily lectionary*)

—*silent reflection*—

CANTICLE OF ZECHARIAH (*see back cover*)

[READING(S) FOR MEDITATION AND REFLECTION

PRAYERS

Prayers of Intercession and Supplication
Risen Christ, even in Lent we celebrate your resurrection each Lord's
day. As your baptized people, we yearn to share more fully in the
paschal mystery which has marked our lives with the sign of the cross.

Hear us as we pray:
   for insight into the implications of our discipleship . . .
   for courage to set our face toward our Jerusalems . . .
   for compassion to meet the needs of others . . .
   for grace to overwhelm our lack of faith . . .
   for faithfulness in what is entrusted to us . . .

We lift up your Church around the world this day.
Cleanse, reform and empower it
   so that we may be channels of your love and justice.

Especially we lift up : . . .

[DWV]

—silent prayer—

[OTHER SELECTED PRAYERS (*see pages 16ff*)

[PRAYERS OF SPECIAL INTENTION (*such as the following*)
   [INTERCESSIONS FOR THE ORDER OF SAINT LUKE (*see back cover*)
   [A COLLECT FOR THE ORDER OF SAINT LUKE (*see p. 248*)

CONCLUDING PRAYER
Almighty God, who fills all things with your presence, we humbly ask you, of your great love, to keep us near to you today; grant that in all our ways and doings we may remember that you see us, and may always have grace to know and perceive what things you would have us to do, and strength to fulfill the same; through Jesus Christ our Lord. **Amen.**

[ADAPTED FROM 5TH C. COLLECT; TAR]

THE LORD'S PRAYER (*see p. 248*)
   (*See UMH 270-271 for musical settings*)

HYMN: [SM; Tune: ST. MICHAEL, *UMH* 372]

> Jesus, we follow Thee,
> in all Thy footsteps tread,
> and pant for full conformity
> to our exalted Head.
>
> We in Thy birth are born,
> sustain Thy grief and loss,
> share in Thy want, and shame, and scorn,
> and die upon Thy cross.

Baptized into Thy death
we sink into Thy grave,
till Thou the quickening Spirit breathe,
and to the utmost save.

Thou said'st, 'Where'er I am
there shall My servant be;
Master, the welcome word we claim
and die to live with Thee.

[No. 130 of Wesley's Hymns on the Lord's Supper]

GOING FORTH
May you be made strong with all strength
that comes from God's glorious power,
and may you be prepared
to endure everything with patience,
while joyfully giving thanks to the One
who has enabled us to share in the inheritance
   of the saints of light,
who has rescued us from the power of darkness
and transferred us into the realm of the beloved Son,
in whom we have redemption, and forgiveness of sins.

(Adapted from Colossians 1:11-13)

Let us bless the Lord.
Thanks be to God! Amen.

Evening Prayer
For Sundays in Lent

ENTRANCE OF THE LIGHT
Light and peace in Jesus Christ.
Thanks be to God.
Return to the Lord your God who is gracious and compassionate, slow
to anger and abounding in love.

(Hebrews 12:2)

HYMN OF LIGHT (*The "Phos hilaron;" see cover 2*)

THANKSGIVING FOR THE LIGHT
Thanks be to you, O Lord,
the Light, the Way, the Truth, the Life;
in you there is no darkness, or death.

You are the Light without which there is darkness;
the Way without which there is wandering;
the Truth without which there is error;
the life without which there is Death.

Lord, say: "let there be Light,"
and I shall see Light, and disdain Darkness;
I shall see the Way and avoid wandering;
I shall see the Truth and shun error;
I shall see Life and escape Death.

Illuminate, O illuminate my soul
which sits in darkness and the shadow of Death;
and direct my feet into the way of peace. **Amen.**

[AUGUSTINE, 4TH C. ALT]

EVENING PRAYER CANTICLE (*see cover 2*)

CONFESSION AND PARDON

O Lord, who gave to your Apostles peace, shed upon us all your holy calm; gather together with your hand all those who are scattered, and bring them like sheep into the fold of your holy Church. Strengthen and confirm us, O Lord, by your Cross, on the rock of faith, that our minds be not shaken by the attacks of the enemy. For you alone are holy.

You know, O Lord, how many and great are our sins, you know how often we sin, from day to day, from hour to hour, in the things we do and the things we leave undone. No more, O Lord, no more, O Lord my God, will we provoke you; no more shall our desire be for anything but you, for you alone are truly lovable. And if again we offend in anything, we humbly ask you of your mercy to grant us strength to find favor again in your sight and to live in a manner more pleasing to you.

[CONFESSION ADAPTED FROM THEODORE STUDITA, 8TH C.; TAR]

—silence—

"This saying is sure and worthy of full acceptance, that Christ Jesus came into the world to save sinners." "If any one sins, we have an advocate with God, Jesus Christ the righteous; and he is the expiation for our sins, and not for ours only but also for the sins of the whole world."
Thanks be to God.

(Pardon from 1 Timothy 1:15 and 1 John 2:1-2)

PSALTER   Psalm 126

    The Lord brings us <u>back</u> to *Zion,*
    we are like dreamers,
      laughing, dancing,
      with <u>songs</u> on our *lips.*
    Other nations say,
      "A new world of wonders!
      The <u>Lord</u> is *with them."*
    Yes, God works wonders.
      Re-<u>joice</u>! Be *glad!*

    Lord, bring us back
      as water to <u>thir</u>-sty *land.*
    Those sowing in tears
      reap, <u>singing</u> and *laughing.*
    They left weeping, weeping,
      <u>casting</u> the *seed.*
    They come back singing, singing,
      holding <u>high</u> the *harvest.*

THE GLORIA (*see back cover*)

SCRIPTURE (*see daily lectionary*)

—silent reflection—

CANTICLE OF MARY (*see front cover*)

[READING(S) FOR MEDITATION AND REFLECTION

PRAYERS

    PRAYERS OF SUPPLICATION AND INTERCESSION
    Holy One, your Christ has been sacrificed for us
      and we keep the feast.
    Like exiles coming home from slavery;
      like hearths cleansed from the leaven of malice and evil;
      like Jonah delivered from the belly of the great fish
        to start his mission anew,
    we celebrate the Paschal feast on the Sundays of Lent.
    Awaiting the great feast of Easter,
      we accept the lighting of the evening lamps as a return to
      Lent's discipline and fasting
      and the renewal of our lives in sincerity and truth.

Stir the penitents to a full return to discipleship
and apostolic witness with your church.
Liberate the catechumens from their thirst, blindness and death.
Make of your whole church a new batch of unleavened bread
to be for the world a sign and foretaste of the new heaven
and new earth.
Bring your church to circumcision of the heart as we prepare
for the Easter Vigil.

[DTB]

—silent prayer—

[OTHER SELECTED PRAYERS (see pages 4ff)

[PRAYERS OF SPECIAL INTENTION (such as the following)
[INTERCESSIONS FOR THE ORDER OF SAINT LUKE (see back cover)
[A COLLECT FOR THE ORDER OF SAINT LUKE (see p. 248)

CONCLUDING PRAYER
Sacrificial God whose gift of love was rejected by people like ourselves: Work in us such true repentance that we may accept your grace, receive your mercy, and live in wonder; praising the perfect sacrifice of the Savior through whom we pray. **Amen.**

[GLH[

THE LORD'S PRAYER (see p. 248)
(See UMH 270-271 for musical settings)

HYMN [77.77; Tune: CANTERBURY, UMH 355]

Forty days and forty nights
you were fasting in the wild;
forty days and forty nights
tempted and yet undefiled:

Sunbeams scorching all the day;
chilly dew-drops nightly shed;
prowling beasts about the way;
stones your pillow, earth your bed.

And if Satan, vexing sore,
flesh or spirit should assail,
you, his vanquisher before,
grant we may not faint nor fail.

So shall we have peace divine;
holier gladness ours shall be;
round us too shall angels shine,
such as ministered to thee.

Keep, O keep us, Savior dear,
ever constant by thy side;
that with thee we may appear
at the eternal Eastertide.

[G.H. SMYTTAN, 1822-1870 AND F. POTT, 1832-1909]

When the office of Compline is not prayed, the Commendation Prayer and the Canticle of Simeon (see pages 10-11) are included here.

GOING FORTH
May the God of the Cross,
who conquered death and promised life,
grant us strength and conviction and bless us
in the name of the holy and blessed Trinity.

[PWC, ALT]

Let us bless the Lord.
Thanks be to God.

Morning Prayer
For Mondays in Lent

CALL TO PRAISE AND PRAYER
O Lord, open my lips,
and my mouth shall proclaim your praise.
Come, let us fix our eyes on Jesus, the author and perfecter of our faith, who for the joy set before him endured the cross, scorning its shame and has taken his seat at the right hand of the throne of God.

(Hebrews 12:2)

HYMN: [87.87 with Refrain; Tune: RESTORATION, *UMH* 340]
Come, ye sinners, poor and needy,
weak and wounded, sick and sore;
Jesus ready stands to save you,
full of pity, love, and power.

Refrain:
I will arise and go to Jesus;
he will embrace me with his arms;
in the arms of my dear Savior,
O there are ten thousand charms.

Come, ye thirsty, come, and welcome,
God's free bounty glorify;
true belief and true repentance,
every grace that brings you nigh.
Refrain

Come ye weary, heavy laden,
lost and ruined by the fall;
if you tarry till you're better,
you will never come at all.
Refrain

Let not conscience make you linger,
nor of fitness fondly dream;
all the fitness he requireth
is to feel your need of him.
Refrain

[JOSEPH HART, 1759]

MORNING PRAYER

Great Spirit, you led Jesus into the wilderness, where he was put to the test. We follow him this day, even in our fear of testing, because he is strong in faith. We are too weak to resist; but in you Christ, our weakness becomes strong, our fears smooth out, our hearts beat steady and firm and true. Loving Spirit, in every time of trouble, may we be found in Jesus, "safe and secure from all alarms." In his name we pray. **Amen.**

PSALTER Psalm 32

Happy the pardoned, whose <u>sin</u> is *fixed*,
in whom God finds no evil, <u>no</u> de-*ceit*.
While I <u>hid</u> my *sin*,
my bones grew weak
  from <u>end</u>-less *groaning*.

Day <u>and</u> - *night*,
under the weight <u>of</u> your *hand*,
my <u>strength</u> - *withered*
as in a <u>sum</u>-mer *drought*.

Then I stopped hiding my sin <u>and</u> spoke *out,*
"God, I confess my wrong." <u>And</u> you *pardoned me.*
No wonder the faithful pray to <u>you</u> in *danger!*
Even a sudden flood will <u>nev</u>-er *touch them.*

You, my shelter, you <u>save me</u> from *ruin.*
You encircle me with <u>songs</u> of *freedom.*
"I show you the <u>path</u> to *walk.*
As your teacher, <u>I</u> watch *out for you.*

"Do not be a stubborn mule,
needing bridle and bit <u>to</u> be *tamed."*
Evil brings grief;
    trusting in <u>God</u> brings *love.*
Rejoice <u>in</u> the *Lord.*
Be glad and sing,
    you <u>faithful</u> and *just.*

THE GLORIA *(see back cover)*

SCRIPTURE   *(see daily lectionary)*

—silent reflection—

CANTICLE OF ZECHARIAH *(see back cover)*

READING(S) FOR MEDITATION AND REFLECTION

PRAYERS
    Prayers of Intercession and Supplication
    Cover us, Lord, with your mercy;
        restrain us from the misuse of money, power, and sex.
    Give us a passion for your reign of compassion and justice
        and the will to love you in all the small duties of this day.
    Restore us to the grace and dignity of our baptism
        and remind us that our work is priestly service.
    As those who live touching another world,
    we bring you this one:
        the holy church on the front lines of martyrdom
            and congregations blinded by trifles . . .
        the nations ravaged by contests of power
            and misuse of wealth and creation's gifts . . .
        those who suffer: the unemployed, the betrayed,
        ` the desperate and depressed . . .
        the needs and cares which rise up in us
            by your Spirit's sighing . . . .

[DTB]

—silent prayer—

[OTHER SELECTED PRAYERS (*see pages 16ff*)

[PRAYERS OF SPECIAL INTENTION (*such as the following*)
  [INTERCESSIONS FOR THE ORDER OF SAINT LUKE (*see back cover*)
  [A COLLECT FOR THE ORDER OF SAINT LUKE (*see p. 248*)

CONCLUDING PRAYER
O One whose glory is revealed through Jesus to his followers: Help us to hear your word and perceive the wonder of divine love. Enable us to grow in grace so that we will descend from the mountain with Christ to the sick and wanting world below; we pray through Christ our Savior. **Amen.**

[GLH]

THE LORD'S PRAYER (*see p. 248*)
  (*See UMH 270-271 for musical settings*)

HYMN: [87.87.87; Tune: CWM RHONODA, *UMH* 127]
Guide me, O thou great Redeemer,
pilgrim through this barren land;
I am weak, but thou art mighty;
hold me with thy powerful hand.
Bread of heaven,
feed me now and evermore.   (*repeat*)

Open now the crystal fountain
whence the healing stream doth flow;
let the fiery cloudy pillar
lead me all my journey through.
Strong deliverer,
be thou still my strength and shield.   (*repeat*)

When I tread the verge of Jordan,
bid my anxious fears subside;
Death of death, and hell's destruction,
Land me safe on Canaan's side.
Songs and praises
I will ever give to thee.   (*repeat*)

[W. WILLIAMS, TR. P. AND W. WILLIAMS]

GOING FORTH
The blessing of the Lord rest and remain upon all God's people, in every land, of every tongue; the Lord meet in mercy all that seek God;

the Lord comfort all who suffer and mourn; the Lord hasten the coming glory, and give us, God's people, the blessing of peace.

[ADAPTED FROM BISHOP HANDLEY MOULE 1841-1920; TAR]

Let us bless the Lord.
Thanks be to God.

Evening Prayer
For Mondays in Lent

ENTRANCE OF THE LIGHT

O God, come to our assistance,

O Lord, hasten to help us.

Thanks be to God.

Christ suffered for us leaving us an example that we might walk in his footsteps. He carried our sins in his body to the cross that we might die to sin and live for justice.

(2 Peter 2:21,24a ICEL)

HYMN OF LIGHT (*The "Phos hilaron;" see cover 2*)

EVENING PRAYER CANTICLE (*see cover 2*)

CONFESSION AND PARDON

God of covenant and grace: you have called us in baptism to be bearers of the Light but we have fallen into the darkness of pride. Like Lucifer, we have wanted to be the Light, full of earthly power and grandeur, revered and praised for our greatness. We have wanted the way of success and the way of magic and ease.

Forgive us when and where we have not been
the Light bearers today:
in jostling for attention . . .
in protecting our position . . .
in deceptive speech . . .
in noise that trumpeted our agenda . . .
In silence now we yield the excesses of our desire and pride to the true light, Jesus Christ.

[DTB]

(a time of silence: letting go and letting Jesus look upon us)

"Let this same mind be in you that was in Christ Jesus,
   who did not regard equality with God
   as something to be exploited,
   but emptied himself, taking the form of a slave
   being born in human likeness."

(Philippians 2: 5-7)

In the name of Jesus Christ we are forgiven
and restored to the Light.
   Thanks be to God.

PSALTER Psalm 17
   Hear my <u>just</u> claim, *God*,
   give me your <u>full</u> at-*tention*.
   My prayer de-<u>serves</u> an *answer*,
   for I <u>speak</u> the *truth*.

   Decide <u>in</u> my *favor*,
   you always see <u>what</u> is *right*.
   You probed my heart,
      tested <u>me</u> at *night*,
   tried me by fire
      but found <u>noth</u>-ing *wrong*.

   Unlike others, I <u>nev</u>-er *lie*.
   I live your word, avoiding violence,
      I walk your path and <u>nev</u>-er *stray*.
   I call to you, God,
      for you <u>an</u>-swer *me*.
   Give me your attention,
      <u>hear</u> me *out*.

   Show me your won-<u>der</u>-ful *love*,
   save the victims
      of those <u>who</u> re-*sist you*.
   Keep a loving <u>eye</u> on *me*.
   Guard me <u>under</u> your *wings*.

   Hide me from those who attack,
      from predators <u>who</u> sur-*round me*.
   They close their heart,
      they <u>mouth</u> con-*tempt*.
   They stalk my path,
      ready to <u>knock</u> me *down*
   like a lion hunting prey,
      <u>waiting</u> in *ambush*.

Rise up, God,
  face them head *on*,
draw your sword and *slay them*,
save me from the *wicked!*
God, use your might
  and cut their lives *short*.

But enrich those you *love*
and give their children plenty
  to pass on to their *young*.
I will then be justified,
  will wake to see your *face*,
and be filled with your *presence*.

THE GLORIA (*see back cover*)

SCRIPTURE (*see daily lectionary*)

—silent reflection—

CANTICLE OF MARY (*see front cover*)

[READING(S) FOR MEDITATION AND REFLECTION

PRAYERS

PRAYERS OF INTERCESSION AND SUPPLICATION
We beg you, Lord,
to help and defend us.

Deliver the oppressed . . .
Pity the insignificant . . .
Raise the fallen . . .
Show yourself to the needy . . .
Heal the sick . . .
Bring back those of your people who have gone astray . . .
Feed the hungry . . .
Lift up the weak . . .
Take off the prisoner's chains . . .

May every nation come to know that you alone are God,
  that Jesus Christ is your child,
    that we are your people, the sheep of your pasture.
[CLEMENT OF ROME, LATE 1ST CENTURY; DTB]

—silent prayer—

[OTHER SELECTED PRAYERS (*see pages 4ff*)

[PRAYERS OF SPECIAL INTENTION (*such as the following*)
  [INTERCESSIONS FOR THE ORDER OF SAINT LUKE (*see back cover*)
  [A COLLECT FOR THE ORDER OF SAINT LUKE (*see p. 248*)

CONCLUDING PRAYER
We humbly pray, O God in heaven, to guide us through the darkness
of this world, to guard us from its perils, to hold us up and strengthen
us when we grow weary in our mortal way; and to lead us by your
chosen paths, through time and death, to our eternal home in your
heavenly kingdom through Jesus Christ our Lord. **Amen.**

[ADAPTED FROM KING'S CHAPEL LITURGY, 1831; DTB]

THE LORD'S PRAYER (*see p. 248*)
  (*See UMH 270-271 for musical settings*)

HYMN [LM; Tune: GIFT OF LOVE, *UMH* 408]
O Christ, you are the Light and Day,
'fore whom the darkness flees away.
You, "very Light of Light," we own,
who has your glorious light made known.

All-holy Lord, to you we bend;
your servants through this night defend.
Oh, grant us calm and quiet night,
then wake us to your morning light.

Asleep though weary eyes may be,
still keep our hearts awake to Thee.
Let your right hand outstretched above
guard those who serve the Lord they love.

Look down, O Lord, our strong Defense;
repress our foes' proud insolence.
Preserve and govern us for good—
whom you have purchased with your blood.

Remember us, dear Lord, we pray,
within this mortal frame of clay.
For you alone our souls defend;
be with us, Savior, to the end.

All laud to God eternally;
All praise, eternal Christ to Thee,
Whom with the Spirit we adore,
Forever and forevermore.

[CHRISTE, QUI LUX ES ET DIES; AN AMBROSIAN HYMN; TRANS. W. J. COPELAND, 1848; ALT DWV]

When the office of Compline is not prayed, the Commendation Prayer and the Canticle of Simeon (see pages 10-11) are included here.

GOING FORTH
O Israel, hope in GOD,
    with whom there is steadfast love,
    and great power to redeem.
It is God who will redeem Israel from all iniquities.

(adapted from Psalm 130:7-8)

Let us bless the Lord.
Thanks be to God.

Morning Prayer
For Tuedays in Lent

CALL TO PRAYER
O Lord, open my lips
and my mouth shall proclaim your praise.
"O God, listen to me.
Be gracious, answer me.
Deep within me a voice says,
"Look for the face of God!"

(Psalm 27:7-8)

HYMN [66.66.888; Tune: RHOSYMEDRE, *UMH* 447]

My song is love unknown,
    my Savior's love to me,
    love to the loveless shown,
    that they might lovely be.
O who am I, that for my sake
my Lord should take frail flesh, and die?
my Lord should take frail flesh, and die?

He came from his blest throne,
   salvation to bestow;
   we turned away and none
   the longed-for Christ would know.
But O, my Friend, my Friend indeed,
who at my need his life did spend!
who at my need his life did spend!

Sometimes they strew his way,
   and his sweet praises sing;
   resounding all the day
   hosannas to their King.
Then 'Crucify!' is all their breath,
and for his death they thirst and cry.
and for his death they thirst and cry.

Why, what has my Lord done?
What makes this rage and spite?
   He made the lame to run,
   he gave the blind their sight.
Sweet injuries! Yet they at these
themselves displease, and 'gainst him rise;
themselves displease, and 'gainst him rise.

They rise, and needs will have
   my dear Lord made away;
   a murderer they save,
   the Prince of Life they slay.
Yet cheerful he to suffering goes,
that he his foes from thence might free;
that he his foes from thence might free.

In life, no house, no home
   my Lord on earth might have;
   in death, no friendly tomb
   but what a stranger gave.
What may I say? Heaven was his home;
but mine the tomb wherein he lay;
but mine the tomb wherein he lay.

Here might I stay and sing.
   no story so divine;
   never was love, dear King,
   never was grief like thine!
This is my Friend, in whose sweet praise
I all my days could gladly spend;
I all my days could gladly spend.   [S. CROSSMAN, 1624-1683]

MORNING PRAYER

Jesus, we confess you, our Savior, Messiah, Priest and Lord.
For us you did all things well.
For us you intercede in love and liberation
   at the right hand of God.
For us you discipline our affections and loyalties
   so we may be healed.
Cheer us as you lead us through the desert
   of these forty days. **Amen.**

[DTB]

PSALTER Psalm 137:1-6

By the rivers of Babylon
   we sat weeping, re-<u>member</u>-ing *Zion.*
There on the poplars
   we <u>hung</u> our *harps.*
Our captors shouted
   for happy songs,
   for <u>songs</u> of *festival.*
"Sing!" they cried,
   "the <u>songs</u> of *Zion."*

How could we sing
   the song of the Lord
   in a <u>for</u>-eign *land?*
Jerusalem forgotten?
   <u>Wither</u> my *hand!*
Jerusalem forgotten?
   <u>Silence</u> my *voice!*
if I do not seek you
   as my <u>great</u>-est *joy.*

THE GLORIA (*see back cover*)

SCRIPTURE (*see daily lectionary*)

—*silent reflection*—

CANTICLE OF ZECHARIAH (*see back cover*)

[READING(S) FOR MEDITATION

PRAYERS

PRAYERS OF SUPPLICATION AND INTERCESSION

Lord God, whom we love and whom we desire to love more,
  bring us to love you as much as we ought.
Come with Christ and dwell in our hearts and keep watch over
  our lips, our steps, our deeds and we shall not need to
  be anxious either for our souls or our bodies.
Give us love that knows no enemy and love that is for others
  as you love us.
Cause our hearts frozen in sin, cold to you and cold to others,
  to be warmed by your divine fire.

[ADAPTATION OF A PRAYER OF ST. ANSELM, DTB]

Hear us as we embrace in the circle of your love:
the life of your church . . .
the world groaning . . .
the cares of our own lives . . .
and those particular concerns which your Spirit prompts
  within us . . . .

[DTB]

—silent prayer—

[OTHER SELECTED PRAYERS *(see pages 16ff)*

[PRAYERS OF SPECIAL INTENTION *(such as the following)*
  [INTERCESSIONS FOR THE ORDER OF SAINT LUKE *(see back cover)*
  [A COLLECT FOR THE ORDER OF SAINT LUKE *(see p. 248)*

CONCLUDING PRAYER
Living and dying, Lord, we would be yours;
keep us yours forever,
and draw us day by day nearer to yourself,
until we are wholly filled with your love
and fitted to behold you, face to face. **Amen.**

[ADAPTED FROM A PRAYER BY EDWARD BOUVERIE PUSEY; DTB]

THE LORD'S PRAYER *(see p. 248)*
  (See UMH 270-271 for musical settings)

HYMN [11.8.11.8; Tune: DAVIS, *UMH* 518
    O Thou, in whose presence my soul takes delight,
        on whom in affliction I call,
      my comfort by day and my song in the night,
        my hope, my salvation, my all!

Where dost thou, dear Shepherd, resort with thy sheep,
to feed them in pastures of love?
Say, why in the valley of death should I weep,
or alone in this wilderness rove?

O why should I wander, an alien from thee,
or cry in the desert for bread?
Thy foes will rejoice when my sorrows they see,
and smile at the tears I have shed.

Restore, my dear Savior, the light of thy face,
Thy soul cheering comfort impart;
and let the sweet tokens of pardoning grace
bring joy to my desolate heart.

He looks! And ten thousands of angels rejoice,
and myriads wait for his word.
He speaks! And eternity, filled with his voice,
re-echoes the praise of the Lord.

[JOSEPH SWAIN, 1791 (Ps. 23)]

GOING FORTH

Blessed be the God and Father of our Lord Jesus Christ, the Father of mercies and the God of all consolation, who consoles us in all our affliction so we may be able to console those who are in any affliction.

(2 Corinthians 1:3-4)

Let us bless the Lord.
Thanks be to God.

Evening Prayer
For Tuesdays in Lent

ENTRANCE OF THE LIGHT

O God, come to our assistance.
O Lord, hasten to help us.
Wait for God; be strong and let your heart take courage.

(Psalm 27:14)

HYMN OF LIGHT (*The "Phos hilaron;" see cover 2*)

[EVENING PRAYER CANTICLE (*see cover 2*)

CONFESSION AND PARDON

O God, pardon our offenses,
done voluntarily or involuntarily, wittingly, or unwittingly,
by word or deed or in thought;
forgive those that are hidden and those that are manifest,
those which were done long ago,
and those done this day;
those which are known;
and those which are forgotten, but are known to you.
Forgive us, O God, through Jesus Christ our Lord. **Amen.**

[FROM THE LITURGY OF SYRIAN JACOBITES]

—silent confession—

If you, O God, should mark iniquities,
  Lord, who could stand?
But there is forgiveness with you,
  so that you may be worshipped.

(Psalm 130:3-4)

Through Christ, we are forgiven.
  Thanks be to God!

PSALTER Psalm 27

I

The Lord is my saving light;
  whom <u>should</u> I *fear?*
God is my fortress;
  what <u>should</u> I *dread?*
When the violent come at me
  to <u>eat me</u> a-*live,*
a mob eager to kill-
  they waver, <u>they</u> col-*lapse.*

Should bat-<u>talions</u> lay *siege,*
I <u>will</u> not *fear;*
should war <u>rage</u> a-*gainst me,*
even then <u>I</u> will *trust.*

One thing I ask the Lord,
  one <u>thing</u> I *seek:*
to live in the house of God
  every day <u>of</u> my *life,*
caught up <u>in</u> God's *beauty,*
at prayer <u>in</u> [his]* *temple.*

(*Recommended alternative:
"God's;" ICEL ="his")

The Lord will <u>hide</u> me *there,*
hide my life <u>from</u> at-*tack:*
a sheltering <u>tent</u> a-*bove me,*
a firm <u>rock</u> be-*low.*

I am now <u>be</u>-yond *reach*
of those <u>who</u> be-*siege me.*
In his temple I will offer
  a <u>joy</u>-ful *sacrifice,*
I will play and <u>sing</u> to *God.*

II

O God, <u>listen</u> to *me;*
be <u>gra</u>-cious, *answer me.*
Deep within me <u>a</u> voice *says,*
"Look for the <u>face</u> of *God!"*

So I look <u>for</u> your *face,*
I beg you <u>not</u> to *hide.*
Do not shut me <u>out</u> in *anger,*
help <u>me</u> in-*stead.*

Do not a-<u>bandon</u> or de-*sert me,*
my <u>savior,</u> my *God.*
If my <u>parents</u> re-*jected me,*
still God would <u>take</u> me *in.*

Teach me <u>how</u> to *live,*
lead me on the right road
  away <u>from</u> my *enemies.*
Do not leave me <u>to</u> their *malice;*
liars breathing violence
  rise to <u>swear</u> a-*gainst me.*

I know I will see
  how <u>good</u> God *is*
while I am <u>still</u> *alive.*
Trust in the <u>Lord.</u> Be *strong.*
Be brave. Trust <u>in</u> the *Lord.*

THE GLORIA *(see back cover)*

SCRIPTURE *(see daily lectionary)*

—silent reflection—

CANTICLE OF MARY (*see front cover*)

[READING(S) FOR MEDITATION AND REFLECTION

PRAYERS

PRAYERS OF THANKSGIVING AND INTERCESSION

God, our rest: we exhaust ourselves in living and
  we come to the end of the day spent.
Grant us rest in heart and body this night.
Forgive us for forgetting you in the day now ending.
Even in sleep restore our souls to centeredness and contentment.
Deliver us from the demons that keep us agitated and fearful —
  acquisitiveness, fear of loss, and lust for gaining and
  keeping the upper hand.
Bring us to love's rest, and to resolve's practice of mercy and trust.
As the world yields to the setting sun,
  Heal the sick,
  Hug the little ones,
  Reconcile the contentious,
  Break the weapons of war,
  Refresh the church,
  Light candles in the hopeless,
  Feed the hungry,
  Shelter and befriend the homeless,
  Through Jesus, the unflinching Messiah.

[DTB]

—silent prayer—

[OTHER SELECTED PRAYERS (*see pages 4ff*)

[PRAYERS OF SPECIAL INTENTION (*such as the following*)
  [INTERCESSIONS FOR THE ORDER OF SAINT LUKE (*see back cover*)
  [A COLLECT FOR THE ORDER OF SAINT LUKE (*see p. 248*)

CONCLUDING PRAYER

God our Savior and Redeemer: you are constantly at work, reaching
out to us in every circumstance. Hear the prayers we make to you,
and continue to bring forth new things in your creation; through Jesus
Christ our Sovereign. **Amen.**

[GLH]

THE LORD'S PRAYER (*see p. 248*)
  (*See UMH 270-271 for musical settings*)

HYMN: [87.87.887; Tune: AUS TIEFER NOT, *UMH* 515]

Out of the depths I cry to you;
O Lord, now hear me calling.
Incline your ear to my distress
in spite of my rebelling.
Do not regard my sinful deeds.
Send me the grace my spirit needs;
without it I am nothing.

All things you send are full of grace;
you crown our lives with favor.
All our good works are done in vain
without our Lord and Savior.
We praise the God who gives us faith
and saves us from the grip of death;
our lives are in God's keeping.

It is in God that we shall hope,
and not in our own merit;
we rest our fears in God's good Word
and trust the Holy Spirit,
Whose promise keeps us strong and sure;
we trust the holy signature
inscribed upon our temples.

My soul is waiting for the Lord
as one who longs for morning;
No watcher waits with greater hope
than I for Christ's returning.
I hope as Israel in the Lord,
who sends redemption through the Word.
Praise God for endless mercy.

[MARTIN LUTHER, 1524; TRANS. BY GRACIA GRINDAL (PS. 130; 120:1-2)]

When the office of Compline is not prayed, the Commendation Prayer and the Canticle of Simeon (see pages 10-11) are included here.

GOING FORTH

Let the word of Christ dwell in you richly;
And whatever you do, in word or deed,
do everything in the name of the Lord Jesus,
giving thanks to God through him.

(Colossians 3:16a-17)

Let us bless the Lord.
Thanks be to God.

Morning Prayer

For Wednesdays in Lent

CALL TO PRAYER
> O Lord, open my lips
> **and my mouth shall proclaim your praise.**
> God be merciful to me, a sinner.

(Luke 18:13)

HYMN   [LM; Tune: GERMANY, *UMH* 427]

> O God of morning and of night,
> we thank you for your gifts of light;
> As in the dawn the shadows fly,
> we seem to find you now more nigh.
>
> Fresh hopes have wakened in the heart,
> fresh force to do our daily part;
> in peaceful sleep our strength restored
> throughout the day to serve you more.
>
> O God of light, your love alone
> can make our human hearts your own;
> Be ever with us, Christ, that we
> may faith-ful, bap-tized people be.

[FRANCIS TURNER PALGRAVE 1824-1897, ALT DWV]

MORNING PRAYER
> Write your blessed name, O Lord, upon my heart,
> there to remain so indelibly engraved,
> that no prosperity, no adversity
> shall ever move me from your love.
>
> Be to me a strong tower of defense,
> a comforter in tribulation,
> a deliverer in distress,
> a very present help in trouble,
> and a guide to heaven
> through the many temptations and dangers of this life. **Amen.**

[THOMAS A KEMPIS, 15TH C.]

PSALTER   Psalm 143

I

> Hear me, <u>faith</u> - ful *Lord!*
> bend to my prayer, <u>show</u> com-*passion.*
> Do not <u>judge</u> me *harshly;*
> in your sight, <u>no one</u> is *just.*

My enemy hunts me down,
  grinding me to *dust,*
caging me with the dead
  in last-ing *darkness.*
My strength drains a-*way,*
my heart is *numb.*

I remember the an-cient *days,*
I recall your wonders,
  the work of your *hands.*
Dry as thir-sty *land,*
I reach out for *you.*

Answer me quick-ly, *Lord.*
My strength is *spent.*
Do not hide from *me*
or I will fall into the *grave.*

Let morning announce your love,
  for it is you I *trust.*
Show me the right way,
  I offer you my-*self.*
Rescue me from my foes,
  you are my only ref-uge, *Lord.*
Teach me your will,
  for you are my *God.*

Graciously lead me, Lord,
  on to lev-el *ground.*
I call on your just name,
  keep me safe, free from *danger.*
In your great love for me,
  dis-arm my *enemies,*
destroy their power,
  for I be-long to *you.*

THE GLORIA (*see back cover*)

SCRIPTURE (*see daily lectionary*)

              —*silent reflection*—

CANTICLE OF ZECHARIAH (*see back cover*)

[READING(S) FOR MEDITATION

PRAYERS

PRAYERS OF THANKSGIVING AND SUPPLICATION
We praise your name, O Lord, for you are faithful and righteous and
spare us from your judgment. We recall your mighty deeds and trust
always in your salvation.
In your steadfast love, hear us as we pray
    for your Church and it's mission . . .
    for the little ones who struggle for their place in this life . . .
    for those who suffer in body, mind or spirit . . .
    for those who seek to follow you . . .
    for those whose needs are known only to you . . .
Teach us to walk in your path and grant us your life.

[GER]

—silent prayer—

[OTHER SELECTED PRAYERS (*see pages 16ff*)

[PRAYERS OF SPECIAL INTENTION (*such as the following*)
    [INTERCESSIONS FOR THE ORDER OF SAINT LUKE (*see back cover*)
    [A COLLECT FOR THE ORDER OF SAINT LUKE (*see p. 248*)

CONCLUDING PRAYER
God of holy love: You offer living water to the world through Jesus.
Keep us close to Christ, that our thirst for righteousness may be
quenched through the Source of our salvation. **Amen.**

[GLH]

THE LORD'S PRAYER (*see p. 248*)
    (*See UMH 270-271 for musical settings*)

HYMN: [8583; Tune: STEPHANOS, *BOH* 99 or BULLINGER, *BOH* 273]
            Art thou weary, art thou languid,
                art thou sore distressed?
            "Come to me," saith One,"and, coming,
                Be at rest."

            Hath He marks to lead me to Him,
                if He be my Guide?
            In His feet and hands are wound prints,
                and His side!

Is there diadem, as Monarch,
that His brow adorns?
Yea, a crown in very surety,
but of thorns.

If I find Him, if I follow,
what reward is here?
Many a sorrow, many a labor,
many a tear!

If I still hold closely to Him,
what hath He at last?
Sorrow vanquished, labor ended,
Jordan passed!

If I ask Him to receive me,
will He say me nay?
Not till earth and not till heaven
pass away!

Finding, following, keeping, struggling,
is He sure to bless?
Saints, apostles, prophets, martyrs,
answer, "Yes!"

[JOHN MASON NEALE, 1818-1866, BASED ON ST. STEPHEN OF MAR SABA, 8TH CENTURY]

GOING FORTH

The time is fulfilled, and the kingdom of God has come near;
repent, and believe in the good news.

(Mark 1:15)

We believe; Lord, help our unbelief!
The grace of the Lord Jesus Christ and the love of God and the *koinonia*
of the Holy Spirit is with us now and always!
Let us bless the Lord.
Thanks be to God.

Evening Prayer
For Wednesdays in Lent

ENTRANCE OF THE LIGHT
O God, come to our assistance.
O Lord, hasten to help us.
Behold, now is the acceptable time,
behold, now is the day of salvation.

(2 Corinthians 6:2)

The Son of Man came not to be served but to serve,
and to give his life as a ransom for many.

(Mark 10:45)

HYMN OF LIGHT (*The "Phos hilaron;" see cover 2*)

[EVENING PRAYER CANTICLE (*see cover 2*)

CONFESSION AND PARDON
God of mercy and judgment who calls us to fast and pray:
We confess the ingratitude of our hearts
  and all the ways we try to improve upon the life you give us:
  -our complicating simple gifts,
  -our impatience with grace unfolding,
  -our demanding of life on our terms,
  -our lack of hospitality for unexpected visitations and surprises.
We repent of our lack of trust and gratitude.
Give us grace to fast from hurry
  and to discover the immense simplicity of things
  through Jesus Christ our Lord.

[DTB]

—silence—

"Listen! I am standing at the door knocking; if you hear my voice
and open the door, I will come into you and eat with you, and you
with me."

(Revelation 3:20)

We are forgiven and released from captivity.
Thanks be to God!

PSALTER Psalm 103

My soul, <u>bless</u> the *Lord,*
bless God's <u>ho</u>-ly *name!*
My soul, <u>bless</u> the *Lord,*
hold dear <u>all</u> God's *gifts!*

Bless God, who forgives your sin
    and <u>heals</u> every *illness*,
who snatches you from death,
    and enfolds you with <u>ten</u>-der *care*,
who fills your <u>life</u> with *richness*
and gives you an <u>ea</u>-gle's *strength*.

The Lord, who works justice
    and de-<u>fends</u> the op-*pressed*,
teaches Moses and Israel
    divine <u>ways</u> and *deeds*.
The Lord is tender and caring,
    slow to anger, <u>rich</u> in *love*.
God will not accuse us long,
    nor bring our sins to trial,
    nor exact from us in kind
    what our <u>sins</u> de-*serve*.

As high as heaven above earth,
    so great is God's <u>love</u> for be-*lievers*.
As far as east from west,
    so God re-<u>moves</u> our *sins*.
As tender as father to child,
    so gentle is <u>God</u> to be-*lievers*.
The Lord knows how we are made,
    remembers <u>we</u> are *dust*.

Our days pass <u>by</u> like *grass*,
our prime like a <u>flower</u> in *bloom*.
A wind comes, the <u>flow</u>-er *goes*,
empty <u>now</u> its *place*.

God's love is <u>from</u> all *ages*,
God's justice beyond all time
    for believers of each <u>gen</u>-er-*ation:*
those who <u>keep</u> the *covenant*,
who take care to <u>live</u> the *law*.

The Lord <u>reigns</u> from *heaven*,
rules over <u>all</u> there *is*.
Bless the <u>Lord</u>, you *angels*,
strong and quick to obey,
    attending <u>to</u> God's *word*.

Bless the <u>Lord</u>, you *powers*,
eager to <u>serve</u> God's *will*.
Bless the Lord, you creatures,
   everywhere <u>under</u> God's *rule*.
My soul, <u>bless</u> the *Lord!*

THE GLORIA (*see back cover*)

SCRIPTURE (*see daily lectionary*)

         —silent reflection—

CANTICLE OF MARY (*see front cover*)

[READING(S) FOR MEDITATION AND REFLECTION

PRAYERS

PRAYERS OF THANKSGIVING AND SUPPLICATION
God of the covenant: We give you thanks this day that we are numbered among your sons and daughters. Through Christ you made us as numerous as the stars of the sky, and by your Spirit you empower us for your work.

We pray this day for those who are tempted to give
   up hope in your promise . . .
For the sick in mind, body, or spirit, that they may be
   succored by the knowledge of your Presence . .
For all outcasts and those without home or land, that
   a place of refuge, shelter, and belonging will soon be theirs . . .
For all who lead the nations, that,
   relying not upon their own strength,
   they may lift their minds above the things of earth
   and focus upon the agenda of heaven . . .

Grant that we in your Church may be responsible citizens of your heavenly country. Forbid that we should become so familiar with the call of Christ that we ignore His claim upon our lives. Shape our endeavors to coincide with your desires. As you lead us toward the land you have promised, send forth your Spirit to guide us on our journey. May what we do be cause for rejoicing, and who we are reflect your radiance: we pray through Jesus Christ, the author of our faith. **Amen.**

[GLH]

—silent prayer—

[OTHER SELECTED PRAYERS *(see pages 4ff)*

[PRAYERS OF SPECIAL INTENTION *(such as the following)*
  [INTERCESSIONS FOR THE ORDER OF SAINT LUKE *(see back cover)*
  [A COLLECT FOR THE ORDER OF SAINT LUKE *(see p. 248)*

CONCLUDING PRAYER
Thanks be to you, O Lord Jesus Christ,
for all the benefits which you have given us;
for all the pains and insults which you have borne for us.

O most merciful Redeemer, friend and brother,
may we know you more clearly,
love you more dearly,
and follow you more nearly, for your own sake. **Amen.**

[RICHARD OF CHICHESTER, 13TH C.]

THE LORD'S PRAYER *(see p. 248)*
  (See UMH 270-271 *for musical settings)*

HYMN: [LMD; Tune: CANDLER, *UMH* 386;
        repeating the last two lines of each stanza]

Come, O thou Traveler unknown,
whom still I hold, but cannot see;
my company before is gone,
and I am left alone with thee;
with thee all night I mean to stay,
and wrestle till the break of day.

I need not tell thee who I am,
My misery and sin declare.
Thyself hast called me by my name;
look on thy hands, and read it there!
But who, I ask thee, who art thou?
Tell me thy Name, and tell me now.

In vain thou strugglest to get free;
I never will unloose my hold.
Art thou the One that died for me?
The secret of thy love unfold:
wrestling, I will not let thee go,
till I thy Name, thy nature know.

Yield to me now, for I am weak,
but confident in self-despair.
Speak to my heart, in blessings speak,
be conquered by my instant prayer:
speak, or thou never hence shalt move,
and tell me if thy Name is Love?

'Tis Love! 'tis Love! Thou diedst for me!
I hear thy whisper in my heart!
The morning breaks, the shadows flee;
pure universal Love thou art;
To me, to all, thy mercies move;
thy nature and thy Name is Love.

My prayer hath power with God; the grace
unspeakable I now receive;
through faith I see thee face to face,
I see thee face to face, and live!
In vain I have not wept and strove-
thy nature, and thy name is Love.

I know thee, Savior, who thou art,
Jesus, the feeble sinner's friend;
nor wilt thou with the night depart,
but stay and love me to the end:
Thy mercies never shall remove,
thy nature, and thy name is Love.

[CHARLES WESLEY, 1707-1788(based on Genesis 32:24-30)]

*When the office of Compline is not prayed, the Commendation Prayer and the
Canticle of Simeon (see pages 10-11) are included here.*

GOING FORTH
May God in the plenitude of love
pour upon you torrents of grace,
bless you and keep you in holy fear,
open to you the paschal mystery,
and receive you at last into eternal glory.

[ADAPTED BLESSING FROM THE CONSECRATION OF COVENTRY CATHEDRAL; TAR; DWV]

Let us bless the Lord.
Thanks be to God.

Propers of the Day

For Holy Week

Vígíl

For the evening before Palm/Passion Sunday

(In keeping with the tradition of the Eastern Church, the prayers and readings for this office focus on the healing of Lazarus)

ENTRANCE OF THE LIGHT
   Light and peace in Jesus Christ.
   Thanks be to God.
   Jesus cried with a loud voice "Lazarus, come out."
   And he said to them, "Unbind him and let him go."

(Adapted from John 11:43-44)

HYMN OF LIGHT (The *"Phos hilaron;"* see front cover)

THANKSGIVING FOR THE LIGHT
   Thanks be to you, O Lord,
   the Light, the Way, the Truth, the Life;
   in you there is no darkness, or death.

   You are the Light without which there is darkness;
   the Way without which there is wandering;
   the Truth without which there is error;
   the life without which there is Death.

   Lord, say: "let there be Light,"
   and I shall see Light, and disdain Darkness;
   I shall see the Way and avoid wandering;
   I shall see the Truth and shun error;
   I shall see Life and escape Death.

   Illuminate, O illuminate my soul
   which sits in darkness and the shadow of Death;
   and direct my feet into the way of peace. **Amen.**

[AUGUSTINE, 4TH C. ALT]

[EVENING PRAYER CANTICLE (selected from Psalm 141)
   A. CHANT FORM: *(see front cover)*
(See UMH, bottom of p. 850 for a musical setting of the antiphon by Arlo Duba)
   B. METRICAL FORM:
               [8888.88; Tune: ST. PETERSBURG *UMH* 153]

               Come quickly, Lord, I call on you;
               And hear my voice, my cry for help.
               Control my lips and tongue, O Lord,
               And save my heart from evil's grasp

Let my prayer rise like incense, Lord,
My hands, an ev'ning sacrifice.

Help me accept rebuke as grace,
And guard me from all bitterness.
All wicked ways may I resist
And never share in sensuous feasts.
Let my prayer rise like incense, Lord,
My hands, an ev'ning sacrifice.

Protect me from the Evil One,
And rule my life through Christ your Son,
With Holy Fire my sins consume,
And flood my soul with love divine,
My heart shall rise as incense, Lord,
My life, your living sacrifice.

[SF]

CONFESSION AND PARDON

Holy God, we believe in you and in your Son, the savior of the world,
    but we have accused him of coming too late to help us.
Like Martha and Mary in the days before Easter,
    our hearts, if not our lips, lament, "Lord, if only you had been here."
Like the sisters of Lazarus, we fail to connect our confession of faith
    with the hurts and hopes of daily life.
Like the crowd of mourners in Bethany we believe in your love,
    but persist in resignation to death's sway.
In the week ahead that we call "Holy,"
    bring us to encounter Jesus in death and in life.
Have mercy upon us and bring us to fullness of faith
    and to everlasting life by him who is the resurrection and the life.

[DTB]

—a time of silent recollection—

Hear the good news: "Who is to condemn? It is Christ Jesus, who
died, yes, who was raised for us. Neither death, nor life, nor things
present, nor things to come, nor powers, nor height, nor depth, nor
anything else in all creation will be able to separate us from the love
of God in Jesus Christ our Lord." In the name of Jesus Christ we are
forgiven and walk in the confidence of everlasting life.

(quotation adapted from Romans 8:34, 38-39)

Thanks be to God!

THE BLESSING

Lord, grant us your blessing.
Let us pray:
Kindle in our hearts, O God,
  the flame of that love which never ceases,
  that it may burn in us, giving light to others.
May we shine for ever in your temple,
  set on fire with your eternal light,
  even your Son Jesus Christ,
  our Saviour and our Redeemer. **Amen.**

[St. Columba, CCP]

PSALTER Psalm 70

Help me, God.
  Lord, be <u>quick</u> to *save me.*
People are plotting to kill me;
  <u>humble</u> them, *shame them.*
They want to ruin me;
  <u>ruin</u> and dis-*grace them.*
Let those who jeer at me
  swallow their <u>shame</u>-ful *taunts.*
But those who seek you
  and trust your <u>sav</u>-ing *love*
rejoice and always sing,
  "<u>God</u> is *great.*"
I am poor and helpless,
  O God, hurry <u>to</u> my *side!*
Lord, my help, my rescue,
  do <u>not</u> de-*lay.*

THE GLORIA (*see back cover; musical setting, UMH 72; or:*)

Glory to God, Love abounding be-<u>fore</u> all *ages;*
Glory to God, Love shown forth in the self-emptying of <u>Je</u>-sus *Christ;*
Glory to God, Love poured out through the <u>gift</u> of the *Spirit,*
  who fashions and renews the <u>face</u> of the *earth;*
Glory to the holy and <u>bless</u>-ed *Trinity!*
All things abiding in Love,
  Love abiding <u>in</u> all *things,*
As it is now, <u>ev</u>-er *was,*
  And ever shall be for endless ages. <u>A</u>-*men.*

[DNP]

SCRIPTURE John 11:1-53

—silent reflection—

CANTICLE OF REDEMPTION (*De Profundis; see page 13*)

[READING(S) FOR MEDITATION AND REFLECTION

PRAYERS
    PRAYERS OF INTERCESSION AND SUPPLICATION
    God of the hard places where death is as common as sleep,
      and resignation is as thick as the sickened tongue,
     come to the Lazarus in us, your church, and waken us
     to the glory of God.
    With Jesus, your Son, give us vision to see life and death
     in the light of living toward your reign.
    With Jesus, your life giver, send us anew to the places where people
    sleep in graves of fear, hunger, hopelessness, and stilled imagination.
    With Jesus, who raised Lazarus
     and angered of the powers of hell,
     bid us walk with him toward the tomb
     where Hades took a body and discovered God,
     where it took earth and discovered heaven.
              [DTB; the concluding lines include allusions to John Chrysostom's great Easter sermon]

—silent prayer—

[OTHER SELECTED PRAYERS (*see pages 4ff*)

[PRAYERS OF SPECIAL INTENTION (*such as the following*)
  [INTERCESSIONS FOR THE ORDER OF SAINT LUKE (*see back cover*)
  [A COLLECT FOR THE ORDER OF SAINT LUKE (*see p. 248*)

CONCLUDING PRAYER
God of strange sovereignty: even rebellious leaders prophesied the holy cross and Jesus' sacrificial death. In this Holy Week take captive all our rebel selves and fix us upon our savior in undying praise and love. **Amen.**

                                  [DTB]

THE LORD'S PRAYER (*see p. 248*)
  (*See* UMH 270-271 *for musical settings*)

HYMN [11.10.11.10; Tune: INTERCESSOR, *UMH* 517]

       O word of comfort, through the silence stealing,
          as the dread act of sacrifice began.
       O voice, which through the ages interceding
         calls us to fellowship with God again!

O word of hope to raise us nearer heaven,
when courage fails us and when faith is dim!
The souls for whom Christ prays to Christ are given,
to find their pardon and their joy in him.

O Intercessor, who art ever living
to plead for dying souls that they may live;
teach us to know our sin which needs forgiving,
teach us to know the love which can forgive.

[ADA R. GREENAWAY, 1861-1937]

When the office of Compline is not prayed, the Commendation Prayer and the Canticle of Simeon (see pages 10-11) are included here.

GOING FORTH

"Let us also go with him that we may die with him" and so believe. May the blessing of holy liturgy and godly imagination accompany us this week and bring us to a holy Easter and to everlasting life. The blessing of the Triune God (+) be upon us.

[DTB]

Let us bless the Lord.
Thanks be to God.

Morning Prayer

For Palm/Passion Sunday

CALL TO PRAYER

O Lord, open my lips
and my mouth shall proclaim your praise.
Lift up your heads, O gates! and be lifted up, O ancient doors!
that the King of glory may come in.

(Psalm 24:7)

HYMN [LM; Tune: THE KING'S MAJESTY *BOH* 425]

Ride on! Ride on in majesty!
Hark! all the tribes Hosanna cry.
O savior meek, pursue Thy road
with palms and scattered garments strowed.

Ride on! Ride on in majesty!
in lowly pomp ride on to die.
O Christ, Thy triumphs now begin
o'er captive death and conquered sin.

Ride on! Ride on in majesty!
The winged squadrons of the sky
look down with sad and wondering eyes
to see the approaching sacrifice.

Ride on! Ride on in majesty!
in lowly pomp ride on to die.
Bow Thy meek head to mortal pain,
Then take, O God, Thy pow'r and reign.

[HENRY HART MILMAN, 1791-1868]

MORNING PRAYER

God whose Christ was given to be the Savior of your people: As he courageously entered Jerusalem, grant that we may with boldness and faith proclaim your salvation to all; through the same Jesus our Redeemer. **Amen.**

[GLH]

CANTICLE Psalm 118: 19-29

Open the gates of justice,
let me praise <u>God</u> with-*in them.*
This is the Lord's own gate,
only the <u>just</u> will *enter.*
I thank you <u>for</u> you *answered me,*

and you be-<u>came</u> my *savior.*
The stone the builders rejected
   has be-<u>come</u> the *cornerstone.*
This is the work of the Lord,
   how wonderful <u>in</u> our *eyes.*
This is the day the Lord made,
   let us rejoice <u>and</u> be *glad.*
Hosanna-save us!
   Lord, <u>grant</u> us suc-*cess!*

Blest is the one who comes,
   who comes in the <u>name</u> of the *Lord.*
We bless you from the <u>Lord's</u> - *house.*
The Lord God <u>is</u> our *light:*
adorn the <u>altar</u> with *branches.*

I will thank <u>you</u>, my *God,*
I will <u>praise</u> you *highly.*
Give thanks, the <u>Lord</u> is *good,*
God's love <u>is</u> for *ever!*

THE GLORIA (*see back cover*)

SCRIPTURE (*see daily lectionary*)

                —silent reflection—

CANTICLE The *Sanctus*
   Let us bless the Lord with praises and loud shouts of thanksgiving:
          (*see musical settings in* UMH *pages 19-28*)
   Holy, holy, holy Lord, God of power and might,
   heaven and earth are full of your glory.
    Hosanna in the highest.
   Blest is the one who comes in the name of the Lord.
    Hosanna in the highest!

[READING(S) FOR MEDITATION AND REFLECTION

PRAYERS
PRAYERS OF THANKSGIVING AND SUPPLICATION
We praise you, Almighty God, for the acts of love by which you have
redeemed us through your Son Jesus Christ our Lord, who, on this
day entered the holy city of Jerusalem in triumph, and was proclaimed
as king by those who spread their garments and branches of palm
along his way.

We too celebrate Christ's triumphal entry into the city by lifting our voices in praise and by laying our prayers at your feet. Especially today we pray:

for those who stand aside, silently suspicious of you . . .
for the children who cry "Hosanna," when we will not listen . . .
for those who seek to silence your word and work . . .
for those who have long awaited your coming glory . . .
for those who need your healing presence . . .

[ADAPTED FROM BCP; TAR]

—silent prayer—

[OTHER SELECTED PRAYERS *(see pages 16ff)*

[PRAYERS OF SPECIAL INTENTION *(such as the following)*
  [INTERCESSIONS FOR THE ORDER OF SAINT LUKE *(see back cover)*
  [A COLLECT FOR THE ORDER OF SAINT LUKE *(see p. 248)*

CONCLUDING PRAYER
Everlasting God, who presented Jesus to be welcomed as Messiah on the way to the cross: enable us who have been clothed with Christ's grace in baptism to spread ourselves like coats under his feet and bear witness to his reign in the world. **Amen.**

[BASED ON A LINE FROM ANDREW OF CRETE, 8TH C.; DTB]

THE LORD'S PRAYER *(see p. 248)*
  (See UMH 270-271 for musical settings)

HYMN [6.5.6.5 D, Tune: KING'S WESTON, *UMH* 168]
At the name of Jesus
every knee shall bow,
every tongue confess him
king of glory now:
'Tis the Father's pleasure
we should call him Lord,
who from the beginning
was the mighty Word.

Humbled for a season,
to receive a name
from the lips of sinners,
unto whom he came.
Faithfully he bore it
spotless to the last,
brought it back victorious,
when from death he passed;

Bore it up triumphant,
with its human light,
through all ranks of creatures,
to the central height,
to the throne of Godhead,
to the Father's breast;
filled it with the glory
of that perfect rest.

Name him, Christians, name him,
with love as strong as death,
name with awe and wonder
and with bated breath;
he is God the Savior,
he is Christ the Lord,
ever to be worshiped,
trusted, and adored.

In our hearts enthrone him;
there let him subdue
all that is not holy,
all that is not true.
Crown him as your Captain
in temptation's hour;
let his will enfold you
in its light and power.

Christians, this Lord Jesus
shall return again,
with his Father's glory
o'er the earth to reign;
for all wreaths of empire
meet upon his brow,
and our hearts confess him
king of glory now.

[CAROLINA MARIA NOEL(1870)]

GOING FORTH

It is ourselves that we must spread under Christ's feet, not coats or
lifeless branches or shoots of trees, matter which wastes away and
delights the eye only for a few brief hours. But we have clothed ourselves with Christ's grace, and with the whole Christ—"for as many
of you as were baptized into Christ have put on Christ"— so let us,
like splendid palm branches, be strewn in the Lord's path.

[ANDREW OF CRETE, 8TH C.; LATIN ANTIPHON]

Let us bless the Lord.
Thanks be to God.

Evening Prayer
For Palm/Passion Sunday

ENTRANCE OF THE LIGHT
Light and peace in Jesus Christ.
Thanks be to God.
Blessed is the one who comes in the name of the Lord!
The Lord is God who has given us light.

(Psalm 118:26-27 sel.)

HYMN OF LIGHT (The *"Phos hilaron;"* see front cover)

THANKSGIVING FOR THE LIGHT
Eternal God, uncreated and primal Light, maker of all created things, fountain of pity, sea of bounty, fathomless deep of loving-kindness: lift up the light of your countenance upon us! Shine in our hearts, true sun of righteousness, and fill our souls with your beauty.

Teach us always to keep in mind your teachings, to talk together about them, and own you continually as our Lord and Friend. Govern by your will the works of our hands; and lead us in the right way, that we may do what is well-pleasing and acceptable to you, that through us your holy name may be glorified. To you alone be praise and honor and worship eternally. **Amen.**

[BASIL; 4TH C. ALT]

[EVENING PRAYER CANTICLE (*see front cover*)

CONFESSION AND PARDON
O Lord of life and truth: Hear our confession and transform us with your terrible mercy. We are diminished because we have not been truthful that sin deals death to the world. We have done evil before you and to the poor, the innocent and the powerless. We have done our own will and not yours. We have been only half-hearted in keeping our appointments with you. Because of our poor discipleship, the Church fails to be a visible embodiment of Jesus and his love. Renew in us crucified love, and restore us to your church as a living sign of your reign.

[DTB]

—silence for the examination of conscience—

The Lord is God who has given us light.
Lead the festal procession with branches,
  up to the horns of the altar!

O give thanks to the Lord who is good,
for God's steadfast love endures for ever!

(Psalm 118:27, 29; adapted)

Thanks be to God.

PSALTER: Psalm 103

My soul, <u>bless</u> the *Lord,*
bless God's <u>ho</u>-ly *name!*
My soul, <u>bless</u> the *Lord,*
hold dear <u>all</u> God's *gifts!*

Bless God, who forgives your sin
and <u>heals</u> every *illness,*
who snatches you from death,
and enfolds you with <u>ten</u>-der *care,*
who fills your <u>life</u> with *richness*
and gives you an <u>ea</u>-gle's *strength.*

The Lord, who works justice
and de - <u>fends</u> the op-*pressed,*
teaches Moses and Israel
divine <u>ways</u> and *deeds.*
The Lord is tender and caring,
slow to anger, <u>rich</u> in *love.*
God will not accuse us long,
nor bring our sins to trial,
nor exact from us in kind
what our <u>sins</u> de-*serve.*

As high as heaven above earth,
so great is God's <u>love</u> for be-*lievers.*
As far as east from west,
so God re - <u>moves</u> our *sins.*
As tender as father to child,
so gentle is <u>God</u> to be-*lievers.*
The Lord knows how we are made,
remembers <u>we</u> are *dust.*

Our days pass <u>by</u> like *grass,*
our prime like a <u>flower</u> in *bloom.*
A wind comes, the <u>flow</u>-er *goes,*
empty <u>now</u> its *place.*

God's love is <u>from</u> all *ages,*
God's justice beyond all time
   for believers of each <u>gen</u>-er-*ation:*
those who <u>keep</u> the *covenant,*
who take care to <u>live</u> the *law.*

The Lord <u>reigns</u> from *heaven,*
rules over <u>all</u> there *is.*
Bless the <u>Lord</u>, you *angels,*
strong and quick to obey,
   attending <u>to</u> God's *word.*

Bless the <u>Lord</u>, you *powers,*
eager to <u>serve</u> God's *will.*
Bless the Lord, you creatures,
   everywhere <u>under</u> God's *rule.*
My soul, <u>bless</u> the *Lord!*

THE GLORIA (*see back cover*)

SCRIPTURE (*see daily lectionary*)

              —silent reflection—

CANTICLE OF MARY (*see front cover*)

[READING(S) FOR MEDITATION AND REFLECTION

PRAYERS

   PRAYERS OF SUPPLICATION AND INTERCESSION
   O God whose Son set his face toward Jerusalem: As he did not turn
   from the cross, grant that we will not shrink from our duty as your
   messengers. Prepare us to take up the cross, that we may be disciples
   of our Savior; the same Jesus Christ our Lord.

   Hear our prayers:
     for our friends and family . . .
     for those who feed the hungry, house the homeless,
       clothe the naked, and visit the imprisoned . . .
     for those deprived of dignity . . .
     for people confined by disability or illness . . .
     for those who wrestle with doubt or despair . . .
     for those confronting the mystery of death . . .

for the church's ministries of compassion . . .
for new beginnings in our lives . . .
for our call to discipleship with Christ . . .

[TAR]

—*silent prayer*—

[OTHER SELECTED PRAYERS (*see pages 4ff*)

[PRAYERS OF SPECIAL INTENTION (*such as the following*)
  [INTERCESSIONS FOR THE ORDER OF SAINT LUKE (*see back cover*)
  [A COLLECT FOR THE ORDER OF SAINT LUKE (*see p. 248*)

CONCLUDING PRAYER
O God, compose our spirits to a quiet and steady dependence on thy good providence. Protect us, we beseech thee, and all our friends everywhere this night, and awaken in the morning those good thoughts in our hearts, that the words of our Savior may abide in us and we in him, who taught us when we pray to say: Our Father . . .

[ADAPTED FROM JOHN WESLEY; TAR]

THE LORD'S PRAYER (*see p. 248*)
  (*See* UMH 270-271 *for musical settings*)

HYMN [CM; tune: LAND OF REST, *UMH* 269]

O thou, from whom all goodness flows,
I lift my heart to thee;
in all my sorrows, conflicts, woes,
good Lord, remember me.

When on my aching burdened heart
my sins lie heavily,
thy pardon grant, thy peace impart:
good Lord, remember me.

When trials sore obstruct my way,
and ills I cannot flee,
then let my strength be as my day:
good Lord, remember me.

If worn with pain, disease, and grief
this feeble spirit be,
grant patience, rest, and kind relief:
good Lord, remember me.

And O, when in the hour of death
I bow to thy decree,
Jesus, receive my parting breath:
good Lord, remember me.

[T. Haweis, 1734-1820]

When the office of Compline is not prayed, the Commendation Prayer and the Canticle of Simeon (see pages 10-11) are included here.

GOING FORTH
Passing from one divine feast to another,
from palms and branches,
let us now hasten, O faithful,
to the solemn and saving celebration of Christ's passion.
Let us behold him undergo voluntary suffering for our sake,
and let us lift up our voices to him with thanksgiving:
Fountain of tender mercy and haven of salvation,
O Lord, glory to you!

[Byzantine Vespers]

Let us bless the Lord.
Thanks be to God.

Morning Prayer
For Monday of Holy Week

CALL TO PRAISE AND PRAYER
Answer me, O Lord, for your love is kind;
in your great compassion turn to me.

(Psalm 69:18, BCP)

HYMN [11.10.11.10; Tune: INTECESSOR, *UMH* 517]
Lord, through this Holy Week of our salvation,
which you have won for us who went astray,
in all the conflict of your sore temptation
we would continue with you day by day.

We would not leave you, though our weak endurance
make us unworthy here to take our part;
yet give us strength to trust the sweet assurance
that you, O Lord, are greater than our heart.

You did forgive your own who slept for sorrow,
you did have pity: O have pity now,
and let us watch through each sad eve and morrow
with you, in pray-er and in sol-emn vow.

[W. H. Draper(1855-1933)]

MORNING PRAYER

Lord our God, holy is your name!
Incline our hearts to you
and give us the wisdom of the cross,
so that, freed from sin,
which imprisons us in our own self-centeredness,
we may be open to the gift of your Spirit,
and so become living temples of your love.
Amen.

[Italian Sacramentary]

PSALTER: Psalm 36

I

Sin whispers <u>with</u> the *wicked,*
shares its evil, <u>heart</u> to *heart.*
These sinners shut their eyes
   to all <u>fear</u> of *God.*
They refuse to see their sin,
   to <u>know it</u> and *hate it.*

Their words ring <u>false</u> and *empty,*
their plans ne-<u>glect</u> what is *good.*
They <u>daydream</u> of *evil,*
plot their crooked ways,
   seizing on <u>all</u> that is *vile.*

II

Your mercy, Lord, <u>spans</u> the *sky;*
your faithfulness soars a-<u>mong</u> the *clouds.*
Your integrity towers <u>like</u> a *mountain;*
your justice runs deeper <u>than</u> the *sea.*

Lord, you em-<u>brace</u> all *life:*
How we prize your <u>ten</u>-der *mercy!*
God, your <u>people</u> seek *shelter,*
safe in the <u>warmth</u> of your *wings.*

They feast at <u>your</u> full *table,*
slake their thirst in <u>your</u> cool *stream,*
for you are the <u>fount</u> of *life,*
you give us <u>light</u> and we *see.*

III

Grant mercy always <u>to</u> your *own,*
victory to <u>hon</u>-est *hearts.*
Keep the proud from trampling me,
    assaulting me with <u>wick</u>-ed *hands.*
Let those sinners collapse,
    struck down, <u>never</u> to *rise.*

THE GLORIA (*see back cover*)

SCRIPTURE (*see daily lectionary*)

               —silent reflection—

CANTICLE OF ZECHARIAH (*see back cover*)

[READING(S) FOR MEDITATION

PRAYERS

PRAYERS OF SUPPLICATION AND INTERCESSIOIN
God whose word cannot be broken: with Jerusalem we are stunned
this Holy Week. Like a city overcome with sudden devastation, we
are swept up in the confusion and desolation, wondering what is hap-
pening.

Liturgy, Scripture and song immerse us in the river that flows
    to betrayal and the cross.
The gospel we have tried to make manageable has overturned
    our tables of control.
    The sufferings of Jesus that we try to avoid engulf us.
    The fruitless fig tree withers before the majesty of one
        whose mission is relentless and uncompromised.
Help us with all of your church to watch and pray,
    to behold anew the unfolding scandal
    and the ragged good news of salvation.
Behold with mercy the agonies of the world
    where the suffering of Jesus is being completed, both then and now.
Let the *Via Dolorosa* for us be both acts of devotion and worship
    and of compassion and justice, so that Christ's abundant suffer-
    ings become the world's abundant consolations.

                                       [DTB]

          —silent prayer—

[OTHER SELECTED PRAYERS (*see pages 16ff*)
[PRAYERS OF SPECIAL INTENTION (*such as the following*)
[INTERCESSIONS FOR THE ORDER OF SAINT LUKE (*see back cover*)
[A COLLECT FOR THE ORDER OF SAINT LUKE (*see p. 248*)

CONCLUDING PRAYER

God of Righteousness: Cleanse your church of impiety, reveal our sinfulness, and enable us to be a holy people who are always ready to proclaim your mighty acts; by the merits of the One who died offering life to all. **Amen.**

[GLH]

THE LORD'S PRAYER (*see p. 248*)
(*See* UMH 270-271 *for musical settings*)

HYMN [66.66.888; Tune: RHOSYMEDRE, *UMH* 447]

My song is love unknown,
my Savior's love to me,
love to the loveless shown,
that they might lovely be.
O who am I, that for my sake
my Lord should take frail flesh, and die?
my Lord should take frail flesh, and die?

He came from his blest throne,
salvation to bestow;
we turned away and none
the longed-for Christ would know.
But O, my Friend, my Friend indeed,
who at my need his life did spend!
who at my need his life did spend!

Sometimes they strew his way,
and his sweet praises sing;
resounding all the day
hosannas to their King.
Then 'Crucify!' is all their breath,
and for his death they thirst and cry;
and for his death they thirst and cry.

Why, what has my Lord done?
What makes this rage and spite?
He made the lame to run;
He gave the blind their sight.
Sweet injuries! Yet they at these
themselves displease, and 'gainst him rise;
themselves displease, and 'gainst him rise.

They rise, and needs will have
my dear Lord made away;
a murderer they save,
the Prince of Life they slay.
Yet cheerful he to suffering goes,
that he his foes from thence might free;
that he his foes from thence might free.

In life, no house, no home
my Lord on earth might have;
in death, no friendly tomb
but what a stranger gave.
What may I say? Heaven was his home;
but mine the tomb wherein he lay;
but mine the tomb wherein he lay.

Here might I stay and sing.
no story so divine;
never was love, dear King,
never was grief like thine!
This is my Friend, in whose sweet praise
I all my days could gladly spend;
I all my days could gladly spend.

[S. CROSSMAN, 1624-1683]

GOING FORTH

Now that you have purified your souls by your obedience to the truth
so that you have a genuine mutual love, love one another deeply from
the heart. You have been born anew.

(1 Peter 1:22-23)

Let us bless the Lord
Thanks be to God.

Evening Prayer

For Monday of Holy Week

ENTRANCE OF THE LIGHT

O God, come to our assistance.
O Lord, hasten to help us.
The Lord is my light and my salvation, whom shall I fear?
The Lord is the stronghold of my life;
of whom shall I be afraid?

(Psalm 27:1)

HYMN OF LIGHT (The *"Phos hilaron;" see front cover*)

[EVENING PRAYER CANTICLE (*see front cover*)

CONFESSION AND PARDON

Holy God, we are afraid of suffering and death. We are afraid of following your Son, because his way leads to a cross. We forget that we will suffer anyway; we forget that in Christ our sufferings can be redemptive. Forgive us. Forgive us especially when our fears turn us away from the pain of other people. Then we deny our own humanity, we deny our suffering Lord, and we deny our sisters and brothers. By the love of Christ, who comes to us when we are troubled, give us a new heart to bear the cross with him.

[DFC]

—silence—

The saying is sure and worthy of full acceptance, that Christ Jesus came into the world to save sinners. If any one sins, we have an advocate with the Father, Jesus Christ the righteous; and he is the atoning sacrifice for our sins, and not for ours only but also for the sins of the whole world.

(1 Timothy 1:15, 1 John 2:1a-2)

Thanks be to God.

PSALTER: Psalm 27

I

The Lord is my saving light;
  whom <u>should</u> I *fear?*
God is my fortress;
  what <u>should</u> I *dread?*
When the violent come at me
    to <u>eat me</u> a-*live,*
a mob eager to kill-
    they waver, <u>they</u> col-*lapse.*

Should bat-<u>talions</u> lay *siege,*
I <u>will</u> not fear;
should war <u>rage</u> a-*gainst me,*
even then <u>I</u> will *trust.*
One thing I ask the Lord,
   one <u>thing</u> I *seek:*
to live in the house of God
   every day <u>of</u> my *life,*
caught up <u>in</u> God's *beauty,*
at prayer <u>in</u> [his]* *temple.*

The Lord will hide me there,
   hide my life <u>from</u> at-*tack:*
a sheltering tent above me,
   a firm <u>rock</u> be-*low.*

I am now beyond reach
   of those <u>who</u> be-*siege me.*
In his* temple I will offer a joyful sacrifice,
   I will play and <u>sing</u> to *God.*

II

O God, <u>listen</u> to *me;*
be <u>grac</u>-ious, *answer me.*
Deep within me <u>a</u> voice *says,*
"Look for the <u>face</u> of *God!"*

So I look for your face,
   I beg you <u>not</u> to *hide.*
Do not shut me out in anger,
   help <u>me</u> in-*stead.*

Do not abandon or desert me,
   my <u>savior,</u> my *God.*
If my parents rejected me,
   still God would <u>take</u> me *in.*

Teach me <u>how</u> to *live,*
lead me on the right road
   away <u>from</u> my *enemies.*
Do not leave me <u>to</u> their *malice;*
liars breathing violence
   rise to <u>swear</u> a-*gainst me.*

I know I will see
 how <u>good</u> God *is*
while I am <u>still</u> a-*live.*
Trust in the <u>Lord</u>. Be *strong.*
Be brave. <u>Trust in</u> the *Lord.*

THE GLORIA *(see back cover)*

SCRIPTURE *(see daily lectionary)*

—silent reflection—

CANTICLE OF MARY *(see front cover)*

[READING(S) FOR MEDITATION AND REFLECTION

PRAYERS
PRAYERS OF INTERCESSION AND SUPPLICATION
O loving Savior, you lead your remnant flock.
O loving Savior, you save your chosen people.
O loving Savior, you feed your wandering followers.
O loving Savior, you plant seeds of new life.
O loving Savior, protect us in the shade of your wings.
O loving Savior, awaken our hunger for you.
O loving Savior, draw us to celebrate your steadfast love.
O mighty God,
  you sent your only-begotten son to free us from all bondage:
  lead us to your holy presence
    that we may be nourished by your abundance.
We pray through your Son, Jesus Christ. **Amen.**

[PWC]

—silent prayer—

[OTHER SELECTED PRAYERS *(see pages 4ff)*

[PRAYERS OF SPECIAL INTENTION *(such as the following)*
  [INTERCESSIONS FOR THE ORDER OF SAINT LUKE *(see back cover)*
  [A COLLECT FOR THE ORDER OF SAINT LUKE *(see p. 248)*

CONCLUDING PRAYER
O God, most merciful, who in the beginning created us, and by the
passion of your only begotten Son has created us anew: Work in us
now, we pray, both to will and to do your good pleasure. And as
much as we are weak, and can do no good thing of ourselves, grant
us your grace and heavenly benediction, that in whatever work we
engage we may do all to your honor and glory; and that, being kept

from sin and daily increasing in good works, so long as we live in the body we may ever show forth some service to you; and after our departure may receive pardon of all our sins, and attain eternal life; through Christ who, with you and the Holy Spirit, lives and reigns for ever and ever. **Amen.**

[ADAPTED FROM ANSELM, 11TH C.; TAR]

THE LORD'S PRAYER *(see p. 248)*
(See UMH 270-271 for musical settings)

HYMN [77.77;Tune: CANTERBURY, *UMH* 355]
Depth of mercy! Can there be
mercy still reserved for me?
Can my God his wrath forbear,
me, the chief of sinners, spare?

I have long withstood his grace,
long provoked him to his face,
would not hearken to his calls,
grieved him by a thousand falls.

I my Master have denied,
I afresh have crucified,
oft profaned his hallowed name,
put him to an open shame.

There for me the Savior stands,
shows his wounds and spreads his hands.
God is love! I know, I feel;
Jesus weeps and loves me still.

Now incline me to repent,
let me now my sins lament.
Now my foul revolt deplore,
weep, believe, and sin no more.

[CHARLES WESLEY, 1740]

When the office of Compline is not prayed, the Commendation Prayer and the Canticle of Simeon (see pages 10-11) are included here.

GOING FORTH
The Lord bless us and keep us.
The Lord be kind and gracious to us.
The Lord look upon us with favor
and give us peace.

(Numbers 6:24-26; alt.)

Let us bless the Lord.
Thanks be to God.

Morning Prayer
For Tuesday of Holy Week

CALL TO PRAISE AND PRAYER
Answer me, O Lord, for your love is kind;
in your great compassion turn to me.

(Psalm 69:18, BCP)

HYMN [88.8886; Tune: ST. MARGARET, *UMH* 480]

O Love that wilt not let me go,
I rest my weary soul in thee;
I give thee back the life I owe,
that in thine ocean depths its flow
may richer, fuller be.

O Light that followest all my way,
I yield my flickering torch to thee;
my heart restores its borrowed ray,
that in thy sunshine's blaze its day
may brighter, fairer be.

O Joy that seekest me through pain,
I cannot close my heart to thee;
I climb* the rainbow thru the rain,
and feel the promise is not vain,
that morn shall tearless be.

O Cross that liftest up my head,
I dare not ask to fly from thee;
I lay in dust life's glory dead,
and from the ground there blossoms red
life that shall endless be.

[GEORGE MATHESON, 1882]

Note: Matheson's original wording="climb"; hymnal text="trace"

MORNING PRAYER
O God of the living: Grant that during this holy week we may find
life eternal in your never failing love and offer ourselves to others as
you have given yourself to us; through Jesus Christ, the gift of life.
Amen.

[GER]

I

Lord, you are my shelter,
  <u>do</u> not *fail me.*
You <u>always</u> do *right;*
de-<u>liver</u> me, *rescue me,*
hear <u>me</u> and *save me.*

Be my rock and haven,
  to whom I can <u>al</u>-ways *turn;*
be my tower of strength,
  <u>keep</u> me *safe.*
The ruthless and <u>wick</u>-ed *trap me;*
reach <u>out</u> to *free me.*

You are my hope, O Lord,
  from the <u>days</u> of my *youth.*
I have relied on <u>you</u> since *birth,*
my strength from my <u>moth</u>-er's *womb;*
I will <u>praise</u> you *always.*

I am shunned like the plague,
  but you keep me <u>in</u> your *care.*
I am filled with your praises,
  all day I <u>sing</u> your *glory.*
Now I am old, my <u>strength</u> - *fails,*
do not <u>toss me</u> a-*side.*

II

My enemies scheme against me,
  they have de-<u>signs</u> on my *life.*
They think God has left me.
  "Strike," they say, "<u>no one</u> will *help.*"
Do not hold back, Lord,
  <u>run</u> to my *rescue.*
Disgrace my accusers,
  wrap them in shame,
  make my enemies
  <u>face</u> utter *ruin.*

I will not lose hope,
  <u>never</u> stop *praising you.*
My lips <u>speak</u> your *goodness,*

praise each day your saving acts,
  though I cannot <u>count</u> them *all.*
I will enter your palace proclaiming,
  "Lord God, you a-<u>lone</u> are *just."*

                              III
From <u>childhood</u> till *now*
you taught me to <u>praise</u> your *wonders.*
Do not <u>leave</u> me, *Lord,*
now that <u>I</u> am *old.*

I can still recount
  to a new generation
  your <u>power</u> and *strength.*
Your <u>goodness</u> is *boundless,*
your <u>works</u> so *great;*
who <u>can</u> - *equal you?*

You <u>wrack me</u> with *torment,*
but you give back my life
  and <u>raise me</u> from this *grave.*
You will re-<u>store</u> my *honor*
and wrap me a-<u>gain</u> in *mercy.*

I will thank you, Lord,
  for <u>your</u> true *friendship*
and play the lyre and harp for you,
  the Holy <u>One</u> of *Israel.*
I will sing <u>out</u> with *joy,*
sing of <u>how</u> you *saved me.*

From <u>morning</u> till *night*
I will <u>trumpet</u> your *goodness;*
Those who <u>sought</u> my *ruin*
are de-<u>feated</u> and *shamed.*

THE GLORIA (*see back cover*)

SCRIPTURE (*see daily lectionary*)

                    —*silent reflection*—

CANTICLE OF ZECHARIAH (*see front cover*)

[READING(S) FOR MEDITATION

PRAYERS

Prayers of Intercession and Supplication
Not only our ancestors alone did the Holy One redeem but us as well,
along with them, as it is written: "And God freed us from Egypt."
Therefore, let us rejoice at the wonder of our deliverance: from bondage to freedom, from agony to joy, from mourning to festivity, from
darkness to light, from servitude to redemption.

We pray for your deliverance, O God:
   for those who remain in spiritual and emotional bondage . . .
   for those who long for your joy . . .
   for those who suffer and mourn . . .
   for those who languish in the darkness of loneliness
      and depression . . .
   for all who are in need of your redemption . . .
Prepare us, O God, to sing a new song.

[Adapted from The Passover Haggadah; TAR]

—silent prayer—

[Other Selected Prayers (see pages 16ff)

[PRAYERS OF SPECIAL INTENTION (such as the following)
   [Intercessions for the Order of Saint Luke (see back cover)
   [A Collect for the Order of Saint Luke (see p. 248)

Concluding Prayer
O God of our longing,
you wipe our tears gently with the caress of your love:
lift up our downcast spirits,
that during this Holy Week we may renew our commitment
to love you above all now and always. **Amen.**

[PWC]

The Lord's Prayer (see p. 248)
   (See UMH 270-271 for musical settings)

HYMN [LM; Tune: OLIVE'S BROW, UMH 282]

Lord, Jesus, when we stand afar,
and gaze upon thy holy Cross,
In love of thee whose love we see,
O may we count the world as loss!

When we behold your bleeding wounds,
and the rough way that you have trod,
make us to hate the load of sin
that lays so heavy on our God.

O holy Lord, uplifted high,
with outstretched arms, in mortal woe,
embracing in your wondrous love
the sinful world that lies below,

Give us an ever-living faith,
to gaze beyond the things we see;
and in the mystery of your death
draw us and all now unto thee.

[BISHOP W. WALSHAM HOW, 1823-1897, ALT.]

GOING FORTH
Amid the mysteries and paradoxes of life, may the abounding love of
our God, the unending hope embodied in our Lord and Savior Jesus
Christ, and the divine strength and sustaining comfort of the Holy
Spirit be with us now and always.

[KAW]

Let us bless the Lord.
Thanks be to God.

Evening Prayer
For Tuesday of Holy Week

ENTRANCE OF THE LIGHT
O God, come to our assistance.
O Lord, hasten to help us.
Let us take refuge in you,
and let us never be put to shame.

(Psalm 71:1)

HYMN OF LIGHT (*The "Phos hilaron;" see front cover*)

[EVENING PRAYER CANTICLE (*see front cover*)

CONFESSION AND PARDON

Turn away, O Lord, the fierceness of your wrath,
 and in pity spare your people:
   Lord, have mercy.
O Christ, look upon our groanings,
loose the bands of death, and grant us life:
   Christ, have mercy.
Behold our tears—consider our sighs,
and in pity forgive our sins:
   Lord, have mercy.

[CONFESSION FROM MOZARABIC BREVIARY, 7TH C.; ALT]

—silence—

O Lord, if you marked iniquities, Lord, who could stand? But there is forgiveness with you, that you may be feared. In Christ we are forgiven.

(Pardon from Psalm 130: 3-4)

Thanks be to God.

PSALTER: Psalm 61

I

Hear me, God! I <u>cry</u> - *out,*
listen <u>to</u> my *prayer.*
I call from far away,
   for my <u>cour</u>-age *fails.*
Lead me to a mountain height
   where <u>I can</u> be *safe.*

You are my refuge,
   a tower of strength a-<u>gainst</u> my *foes.*
Welcome me into your home,
   under your <u>wings</u> for *ever.*
God, you surely <u>hear</u> my *vows;*
give me the blessings
   of those who <u>honor</u> your *name.*

II

Lengthen the days of your king,
   stretch <u>years into</u> gener-*ations.*
May he live with you for ever,
   secure in your <u>faith</u>-ful *love.*
I <u>sing your</u> name *always,*
each day ful-<u>filling</u> my *vows.*

THE GLORIA (*see back cover*)

SCRIPTURE (*see daily lectionary*)

—silent reflection—

CANTICLE OF MARY (*see back cover*)

[READING(S) FOR MEDITATION AND REFLECTION

PRAYERS

PRAYERS OF THANKSGIVING AND INTERCESSION
O God, from the time we were in our mothers' wombs, you have been
the One on whom we have leaned. Our praises are continually of you.
As our days pass, you remain steadfast as our strong fortress and refuge. We sing the greatness of your holy Name from of old.

Fill us with the power of your Holy Spirit that we who are weak may
boast of the Lord. Enkindle in us the light of the knowledge of how
you have come to save all of creation and give us the strength to proclaim your greatness to the ends of the earth; assist us to bring the
powerful to worship before your throne.

There are among our concerns this day those who would see Jesus.
Many are in danger of losing their lives to disease; others suffer greatly
because they cannot understand the world around them; persecution
lies heavy on the heads of people we love. Visit them in your mercy,
O God, and deliver them from their distress.

You have glorified your Name, almighty God, and you will glorify it
again. Give us a spirit of glory as you hear and answer us as we pray
in the name of Jesus.

[AAWY: A; TJC; SEL]

—silent prayer—

[OTHER SELECTED PRAYERS (*see pages 4ff*)

[PRAYERS OF SPECIAL INTENTION (*such as the following*)
 [INTERCESSIONS FOR THE ORDER OF SAINT LUKE (*see back cover*)
 [A COLLECT FOR THE ORDER OF SAINT LUKE (*see p. 248*)

CONCLUDING PRAYER
Eternal God, grant me true quietness,
for you are rest and quiet without end.
Eternal light, grant me the abiding light,
that I may live and quicken in your good. **Amen.**

[ANGILBERT, 8TH C.]

THE LORD'S PRAYER *(see p. 248)*
(See UMH 270-271 for musical settings)

HYMN [CM; TUNE: CAMPMEETING *UMH* 492]
All you who seek for sure relief
in trouble and distress,
whatever sorrow vex the mind,
or guilt the soul oppress,

Jesus, who gave himself for you
upon the Cross to die,
opens to you his sacred heart:
O to that heart draw nigh.

You hear how kindly he invites;
you hear his words so blest:
"All you that labor come to me,
and I will give you rest."

O Jesus, joy of saints on high,
o hope of sinners here,
attracted by those loving words
to you we lift our prayer.

Wash thou our wounds in that dear blood
which from your heart does flow;
a new and contrite heart on all
who cry to you bestow.

[18TH C. TR. E. CASWALL]

When the office of Compline is not prayed, the Commendation Prayer and the Canticle of Simeon (see pages 10-11) are included here.

GOING FORTH
May the God of hope fill you with all joy and peace in believing, so
that you may abound in hope by the power of the Holy Spirit.

(Romans 5: 13)

Let us bless the Lord.
Thanks be to God. Amen.

Morning Prayer

For Wednesday of Holy Week

CALL TO PRAISE AND PRAYER
> Answer me, O Lord, for your love is kind;
> **in your great compassion turn to me.**

(Psalm 69:18, BCP)

HYMN [CM; Tune: CRIMOND, *UMH* 118]

O God, I love you, not because
I hope for heaven thereby,
nor yet because who love you not
are lost eternally.

You, O my Jesus, you did me
upon the Cross embrace;
for me did bear the nails and spear,
and manifold disgrace,

And griefs and torments numberless,
and sweat of agony;
yea, death itself—and all for me
who was your enemy.

Then why, O bless-ed Jesus Christ,
should I not love you well?
Not for the sake of winning heaven,
nor of escaping hell;

Not from the hope of gaining aught,
nor seeking a reward;
but as yourself has lov-ed me,
o ever-loving Lord.

So would I love you, dearest Lord,
and in your praise will sing;
solely because you are my God,
and my most loving King.

[17TH C. TR. E CASWALL; ALT DWV]

MORNING PRAYER
> O God, who for our redemption gave your only begotten Son to the death of the Cross, and by his glorious resurrection delivered us from the power of the enemy. Grant us so to live our baptism that we may die daily to sin, and evermore live with you, in the joy of the resurrection; through the same Jesus Christ our Lord. **Amen.**

[ADAPTED FROM GREGORY THE GREAT; TAR]

PSALTER: Psalm 69: 1-17 (spoken)

I

Solo 1:   Save me, God!
Water is up to my neck.
I am sinking in mud,
without a rock to stand on,
plunged in the deep
beneath the current.
I am tired of shouting,
my throat is raw,
my eyes swollen;
I am worn out waiting for God.

Solo 2:   Many hate me without cause,
they outnumber the hairs on my head.
I have fewer bones
than I have lying enemies
who demand I return
what I did not steal.

Unison: God, you know my folly,
my sins are plain to you.

Solo 1:   Lord, commander of heaven's army,
may those who hope in you
not be shamed because of me.
May those seeking you
not be humbled on my account,
Lord God of Israel.

Solo 2:   I bear shame and insult
because I bear your name.
Rejected by my family,
I am a stranger to my kin.
My passion for your cause
takes all my strength.
Insults meant for you
now fall on me.

Solo 1:   Despite my tears and fasting,
I only gained contempt.
My sackcloth made me a joke.
I was the butt of gossips,
the victim of drunkard's taunts.

Unison:	Lord, hear this prayer, favor me now with love, and send me your ready help.
Solo 2:	Lift me from the mud, keep me from sinking, let me escape my tormentors and rise above the waters. Do not let the waters drown me, the deep swallow me, the pit close me in its mouth.
Unison:	Answer me, Lord, turn to me with mercy and love.

THE GLORIA (*see back cover*)

SCRIPTURE (*see daily lectionary*)

—*silent reflection*—

CANTICLE OF ZECHARIAH (*see back cover*)

[READING(S) FOR MEDITATION

PRAYERS

PRAYERS OF SUPPLICATION AND INTERCESSION

Night navigator, cross bearer, gloom shaker, love bidder:
You take us on the Lenten journey to join us to your dying and rising.
We are awe struck that you lead us through deep gloom
  and break our bonds of sin asunder.
We give you thanks for your great mercy and your tough love.
Keep us moving toward the dawn of the empty tomb.
Deliver us from our rebellious ways,
  and put our feet on straight paths.
Quench our thirst with the living water of your Word
  in Scripture, liturgy and contemplation.
Work repentance in us and reconcile us to those we have
  wounded and wronged.
Take from us our addiction to autonomy
  and let us know the joy of communal obedience
  to your coming reign.

[DTB]

—*silent prayer*—

[OTHER SELECTED PRAYERS (*see pages 16ff*)
[PRAYERS OF SPECIAL INTENTION (*such as the following*)
[INTERCESSIONS FOR THE ORDER OF SAINT LUKE (*see back cover*)
[A COLLECT FOR THE ORDER OF SAINT LUKE (*see p. 248*)

CONCLUDING PRAYER

God, Deliverer of Israel: As your Anointed freed us from captivity to sin and death by your mighty power, empower us to work for the liberation of all people; by the merits of Christ our Emancipator. **Amen.**

[GLH]

THE LORD'S PRAYER (*see p. 248*)
    (*See* UMH 270-271 *for musical settings*)

HYMN [77.77D Tune: ABERYSTWYTH, *UMH* 479]

Lord! Thy death and passion give
strength and comfort at my need,
every hour while here I live
on Thy love my soul shall feed.
Doth some evil thought upstart?
Lo, Thy cross defends my heart,
shows the peril, and I shrink
back from loitering on the brink.

Would the world my steps entice
to yon wide and level road,
fill'd with mirth and pleasant vice?
Lord, I think upon the load
Thou didst once for me endure,
and I fly all thoughts impure;
thinking on thy bitter pains,
hush'd in prayer my heart remains.

Yes, Thy cross hath power to heal
all the wounds of sin and strife,
lost in Thee my heart doth feel
sudden warmth and nobler life.
In my saddest, darkest grief,
let Thy sweetness bring relief,
Thou who camest but to save,
Thou who fearest not the grave!

Lord, in Thee I place my trust,
Thou art my defense and tower;
death Thou treadest in the dust,
o'er my soul he hath no power.
That I may have part in Thee
help and save and comfort me,
give me of thy grace and might,
resurrection, life and light.

Fount of Good, within me dwell,
for the peace thy presence sheds,
keeps us safe in conflict fell,
charms the pain from dying beds.
Hide me safe within Thine arm,
where no foe can hurt or harm;
whoso, Lord, in Thee doth rest,
now has conquered and is blest.

[HEERMANN, 1644; TRANS. CATHERINE WINKWORTH IN LYRA GERMANICA, 1868]

GOING FORTH
God forbid that I should glory, save in the Cross
of our Lord Jesus Christ.
In him is salvation, life, and resurrection from the dead.
God be merciful to us, and bless us, and shine your
divine countenance upon us.

[ADAPTED FROM SCRIPTURE; WPM]

Let us bless the Lord.
Thanks be to God.

Evening Prayer
For Wednesday of Holy Week

ENTRANCE OF THE LIGHT
O God, come to our assistance.
O Lord, hasten to help us.
Unless a grain of wheat falls into the earth and dies, it remains alone;
but if it dies, it bears much fruit.

(John 12:24)

HYMN OF LIGHT (*The "Phos hilaron;" see front cover*)

[EVENING PRAYER CANTICLE (*see front cover*)

CONFESSION AND PARDON

O Christ, the Son of God—so loving, yet hated—so forbearing, yet assaulted unto death—who showed yourself merciful to your persecutors; grant that through the wounds of your passion our sins may be forgiven, and as in your humiliation you suffered death for us, so now, being glorified, bestow on us everlasting brightness.

[MOZARABIC LITURGY, 7TH C.]

—silence for confession—

We who once were estranged and hostile in mind, doing evil deeds, Christ has now reconciled in his body of flesh by his death, in order to present us holy and blameless and irreproachable before God. In the crucified and risen Christ, we are forgiven.

(Colossians 1:21-22)

Thanks be to God.

PSALTER Psalm 41

Blest are those ready to <u>help</u> the *poor;*
in hard times God re-<u>pays</u> their *care.*
God watches, protects,
 blesses them in their land,
 lets no enemy <u>swallow</u> them *up!*
God comforts them on their sickbed
 and nurses <u>them</u> to *health.*

I said, "God, pity me,
 heal me for <u>I</u> have *failed you."*
Enemies predict the worst for me:
 "How soon till this one dies,
 how <u>soon</u> for-*gotten?"*
Visitors all <u>wish</u> me *well,*
but they come seeking bad news
 to gossip <u>on</u> the *street.*

My enemies whisper
 and spread the <u>worst</u> a-*bout me:*
"Something fatal has taken hold,
 this one will <u>not</u> get *well."*
Even my <u>trust</u>-ed *friend*
who used to eat with me
 now <u>turns</u> on *me.*

Pity me, God, restore me
   so I can <u>pay</u> them *back.*
Then I will know you favor me
   when my foes can-<u>not</u> pre-*vail.*
I am innocent; uphold me!
   Let me stand with <u>you</u> for *ever.*
Blessed be the Lord,
   God of Israel for ever.
   A-<u>men</u>! A-*men!*

THE GLORIA (*see back cover*)

SCRIPTURE (*see daily lectionary*)

—silent reflection—

CANTICLE OF MARY (*see front cover*)

[READING(S) FOR MEDITATION AND REFLECTION

PRAYERS

PRAYERS OF INTERCESSION AND SUPPLICATION
Save us, O God, and raise us up by your Christ.

Let us beg for the mercies of the Lord, and for God's compassion . . .
for the angel of peace . . .
for those things which are good . . .
for a Christian departure out of this life . . .
for an evening and a night of peace, and free from sin . . .
and let us beg that the whole course of our life
   glorify our Savior Jesus Christ.

—silent prayer—

O Living God, we dedicate ourselves and one another to you
through Christ our Lord. **Amen.**

[ADAPTED FROM APOSTOLIC CONSTITUTIONS, 4TH C.; TAR]

[OTHER SELECTED PRAYERS (*see pages 4ff*)

[PRAYERS OF SPECIAL INTENTION (*such as the following*)
  [INTERCESSIONS FOR THE ORDER OF SAINT LUKE (*see back cover*)
  [A COLLECT FOR THE ORDER OF SAINT LUKE (*see p. 248*)

God of mercy: look down on your family, for whose sake our Lord Jesus Christ did not hesitate to be betrayed into the hands of the wicked and to undergo the torment of the cross. Renew us by your Spirit in these holy days that we might serve you faithfully, through the same Jesus Christ our Lord. **Amen.**

[ROMAN RITE; ALT DWV]

THE LORD'S PRAYER *(see p. 248)*
(See UMH 270-271 for musical settings)

HYMN [665.665.786; Tune: JESU, MEINE FREUDE, *UMH* 532]
Jesus, priceless treasure,
Source of purest pleasure,
Truest friend to me,
Long my heart hath panted,
Till it well nigh fainted,
Thirsting after thee.
Thine I am, O spotless Lamb,
I will suffer naught to hide thee,
Ask for naught beside thee.

In thine arms I rest me;
Foes who would molest me
Cannot reach me here.
Though the earth be shaking,
Every heart be quaking,
Jesus calms our fear;
Sin and hell in conflict fell
With their heaviest storms assail us;
Jesus will not fail us.

Hence, all thoughts of sadness!
For the Lord of gladness,
Jesus, enters in.
Those who love the Father,
Though the storms may gather,
Still have peace within;
Yea, what e'er we here must bear,
Still in thee lies purest pleasure,
Jesus, priceless treasure!

[JOHANN FRANK, 1653; TRANS. BY CATHERINE WINKWORTH, 1863]

When the office of Compline is not prayed, the Commendation Prayer and the Canticle of Simeon (see pages 10-11) are included here.

GOING FORTH

The Lord Jesus Christ be near to defend us, within to refresh us, around to preserve us, before to guide us, behind to justify us, above to bless us; who lives and reigns with you and the Holy Spirit, one God for evermore.
Let us bless the Lord.
Thanks be to God.

[ANONYMOUS, 10TH C.]

Morning Prayer
For Thursday of Holy Week

CALL TO PRAYER

The first fruits of the Lord's Passion fill this present day with light. Come then, all who love to keep the feast, and let us welcome it with songs, for the Creator draws near to undergo the cross.

[BYZANTINE MATINS]

"Where is my guest room where I may eat the Passover with my disciples?"

(Mark 14:14)

HYMN [LM; Tune: ROCKINGHAM, *UMH* 299]

The heavenly Word proceeding forth,
yet leaving not the Father's side,
went forth unto his work on earth
until he reached life's eventide.

By false disciple to be given
to foemen for his death athirst,
himself the Bread of life from heaven,
he gave to his disciples first.

By birth their fellow-man was he;
their meat, when sitting at the board;
he died, their ransomer to be;
he ever reigns, their great reward.

O saving Victim, opening wide
the gate of heaven to us below,
our foes press on from every side;
thine aid supply, thy strength bestow.

All praise and thanks to thee ascend
for evermore, blest One in Three;
O grant us life that shall not end
in our true native land with thee.

[Thomas Aquinas (1227-74), Trans. John Mason Neale (1818-66)]

MORNING PRAYER

Jesus, our feet are dirty from the journey. How will we become clean
again? When evening comes, who will make us clean and ready for
the meal? Where will we find the water for these soiled soles? Restore us to the joy of God's salvation. **Amen.**

[DTB]

PSALTER: Psalm 102

Hear my prayer, Lord,
   let my cry - *reach you.*
Do not turn from me
   in my hour of *need.*
When I call, listen,
   answer me at *once.*
For my days dissolve like smoke,
   my bones are burned to *ash.*

My heart withers a-way like *grass.*
I even forget to eat,
   so consumed am I with grief.
   My skin hangs on my *bones.*
Like a gull lost in the desert,
   like an owl haunting the *ruins,*
I keep a solitary watch,
   a lone bird on a *roof.*

All day my enemies mock me,
   they make my name a *curse.*
For bread, I eat ashes,
   tears salt my *drink.*
You lifted me up in anger
   and threw me to the *ground.*
My days pass into evening,
   I wither like the *grass.*

But you, Lord, preside for ever,
   every age re-*members you.*
Rise with mercy for Zion,
   for now is the time for *pity.*

Your servants treasure <u>ev</u>'ry *stone,*
  they cherish <u>even</u> the *rubble.*

Nations will fear your name,
  your glory will <u>hum</u>-ble *kings.*
When you rebuild Zion's walls,
  you will appear in <u>glo</u>-ry, *Lord.*
You hear the <u>home</u>-less *pleading*
and do not <u>mock</u> their *prayer.*

Write this down for those to come,
  a people created to <u>praise</u> our *God:*
"The Lord watches from on high,
  searches the <u>earth</u> from *heaven.*
God hears the prisoner's groan
  and sets the doomed free
  to sing the Lord's name in Zion,
  God's <u>praise</u> in Je-*rusalem.*
There the nations and peoples
  gather to <u>serve</u> the *Lord.*"

God has broken me in my prime,
  has cut <u>short</u> my *days.*
I say: "My God, do not take me.
  My life is only half-spent,
  while you live from <u>age</u> to *age.*"
Long ago you made the earth,
  the heavens, too, <u>are</u> your *work.*
Should they decay, <u>you</u> re-*main.*

Should they wear out like a robe,
  like clothing changed and <u>thrown</u> a-*way,*
you are still the same.
  Your years will <u>nev</u>-er *end.*
May your servants' line <u>last</u> for *ever,*
  our children grow <u>strong</u> be-*fore you.*

THE GLORIA (*see back cover*)

SCRIPTURE (*see daily lectionary*)

—*silent reflection*—

CANTICLE OF ZECHARIAH (*see back cover*)

[READING(S) FOR MEDITATION

PRAYERS
Prayers of Thanksgiving and Supplication
God of Passover, Son of God's passion, Story Weaver: On this day you directed two disciples to follow a man carrying a water jar and so know where to eat the Exodus meal. We bless you that Lent's journey now brings us to the waters of baptism and the Paschal Mystery. Gather us together for story, footwashing and Eucharist so we may proclaim anew the saving deeds of Jesus, your apostle of cross-shaped glory.

> Enfold your church
> > in the central story of your saving deeds in these three days.
> Birth new disciples in the rites of initiation.
> Reconcile penitents with towel, basin,
> > and mutual forgiveness for hurt we have caused one another.
> Draw seekers to observe and wonder at these dramatic acts of
> > your extravagant grace.
> In all our ritualizing and reflection, remember the suffering
> > ones among us and touch them with our hands in your name.

[DTB]

—silent prayer—

[Other Selected Prayers *(see pages 16ff)*

[Prayers of Special Intention *(such as the following)*
  [Intercessions for the Order of Saint Luke *(see back cover)*
  [A Collect for the Order of Saint Luke *(see p. 248)*

Concluding Prayer
O Lord of desert and solitude, O Mystery transforming: we come to the end of these forty days that bring profit to our souls: plunge us now into the mystery of your passion and bring us to the triumph of holy Easter as, by your grace, we pass over from death to life and from sin to the glorious liberty of the daughters and sons of God.
Amen.

[DTB]

The Lord's Prayer *(see p. 248)*
  (See UMH 270-271 for musical settings)

HYMN [87.87; Tune: FOR THE BREAD, *UMH* 614]
> For the bread which you have broken,
> For the wine which you have poured,
> For the words which you have spoken,
> Now we give you thanks, O Lord.

By this pledge that you do love us,
By your gift of peace restored,
By your call to heaven above us,
Hallow all our lives, O Lord.

With our sainted ones in glory
Seated at the heavenly board,
May the church that's waiting for you
Keep love's tie unbroken, Lord.

In your service, Lord, defend us,
In our hearts keep watch and ward;
In the world where you have sent us,
Let your kingdom come, O Lord.

[LOUIS F. BENSON, 1924 (MT. 26:26-29; MK. 14:22-25; LK. 22:15-20)]

GOING FORTH

Blessings as we come to the Triduum and
the shadows and
the cross and
the grave and
the fire and
the book and
the font and
the table and
the Life of all that lives.

May it bring us back to the place that grace and penitence brought us
when we first believed.

[DTB]

Let us bless the Lord.
Thanks be to God.

Propers of the Day For the Triduum

Since the fourth century, the Church has observed the holy triduum (the great three days) of the crucified, buried, and risen Lord. It is the central point of the liturgical year, beginning on Holy Thursday evening, reaching its climax in the Great Vigil of Easter

The church observes these days in a variety of ways. Some congregations come closer to the pattern of the Daily Office during the Triduum than at any other time of the church year. Some of these offices will be replaced by the observances of the congregation of which one is a part. Never-the-less, because few parishes observe all of the Triduum, resources are provided for all of its offices.

Some of these will become "solitary" offices supplementary to the "people's services" or "cathedral offices" of the congregation. Others may be used or adapted by churches for "prayer vigils." A gathered community may choose to observe the complete cycle as it participates in the paschal mystery celebrated by the Triduum.

Solemn Vespers

For Holy Thursday

ENTRANCE OF THE LIGHT
The Love of Christ has gathered us as one.
Let us rejoice and be glad in him.
Let us fear and love the living God,
and in purity of heart let us love one another.
Where charity and love are, there is God.
When therefore we are gathered together
let us not be divided in spirit.
Let bitter strife and discord cease between us;
Let Christ our God be present in our midst.
Where charity and love are, there is God.
With all the blessed may we see forever
your face in glory, Jesus Christ our God,
joy that is infinite and undefiled
for all the ages of eternity.
Where charity and love are, there is God.

[MAUNDY THURSDAY, WESTERN RITE]

HYMN OF LIGHT (*The "Phos hilaron" see front cover; or another hymn*)

[INCENSE

[EVENING PRAYER CANTICLE (*see front cover*)

CONFESSION AND ASSURANCE

THE KYRIE   (*For musical settings, see* UMH 482-484)
Lord, have mercy.
Christ have mercy.
Lord, have mercy.

Psalm 51:1-17

Have mercy, tender God,
forget that I de-*fied you.*
Wash away my sin,
cleanse me from my *guilt.*
I know my evil well,
it stares me in the *face,*
evil done to you alone
before your ve-ry *eyes.*

How right your condemnation!
  Your verdict <u>clear</u>-ly *just.*
You see me for what I am,
  a sinner be-<u>fore</u> my *birth.*
You love those centered in truth;
  teach me your <u>hid</u>-den *wisdom.*
Wash me with fresh water,
  wash me <u>bright</u> as *snow.*

Fill me with happy songs,
  let the bones you <u>bruised</u> now *dance.*
Shut your eyes to my sin,
  make my guilt <u>dis</u>-ap-*pear.*
Creator, reshape my heart;
  God, <u>steady</u> my *spirit.*
Do not cast me aside
  stripped of your <u>ho</u>-ly *spirit.*

Save me, bring <u>back</u> my *joy,*
support me, <u>strengthen</u> my *will.*
Then I will <u>teach</u> your *way*
and sinners will <u>turn</u> to *you.*

Help me, stop my tears,
  and I will <u>sing</u> your *goodness.*
Lord, give me words
  and I will <u>shout</u> your *praise.*

When I offer a holocaust,
  the gift <u>does</u> not *please you.*
So I offer my shattered spirit;
  a changed <u>heart</u> you *welcome.*

—silence—

ASSURANCE
If we confess our sins, God is faithful and just, and will forgive our sins and cleanse us from all unrighteousness. In Christ, we are forgiven.
  Thanks be to God.

(1 John 1:9)

I am <u>filled</u> with *love,*
for the <u>Lord -</u> *hears me;*
the Lord <u>bends</u> to my *voice*
when-<u>ever</u> I *call.*

Death had me <u>in</u> its *grip,*
the grave's trap was set,
   grief <u>held</u> me *fast.*
I cried <u>out</u> for *God,*
"Please, <u>Lord -</u> , *rescue me!"*

Kind and faithful is the Lord,
   gentle <u>is</u> our *God.*
The Lord shelters the poor,
   raises me <u>from</u> the *dust.*
Rest once <u>more,</u> my *heart,*
for you <u>know the</u> Lord's *love.*

God rescues me from death,
   wiping my tears,
   <u>steadying</u> my *feet.*
I walk with the Lord
   in this <u>land</u> of the *living.*
I believe, even as I say,
   "I <u>am</u> af-*flicted."*
I believe, even though I scream,
   "<u>Every</u> - one *lies!"*

What gift can ever repay
   God's <u>gift</u> to *me?*
I raise the cup of freedom
   as I <u>call on</u> God's *name!*
I fulfill my <u>vows</u> to you, *Lord,*
standing before <u>your</u> as-*sembly.*

Lord, you hate to see
   your <u>faithful</u> ones *die.*
I beg you, Lord, hear me:
   it is I, the <u>servant</u> you *love,*
I, the <u>child of</u> your *servant.*
   You freed me <u>from</u> death's *grip.*

I bring a gift of thanks,
  as I <u>call on</u> your *name.*
I fulfill my <u>vows to</u> you, *Lord,*
standing before your assembly,
  in the <u>courts</u> of your *house,*
within the heart of Jerusalem.
  <u>Praise</u> the *Lord!*

SCRIPTURE (*a time of silence follows each reading*)
  Exodus 12:1-14
  1 Corinthians 11: 23-26
  John 13: 1-17

[CANTICLE OF REDEMPTION (*De Profundis; omit if being used
                              as one of the lessons in the Vigil*)
[Psalm Tone Five (for a metrical form, see *UMH* 515)]

  Out of the depths I cry to you, O God;
    Lord, <u>hear</u> my *voice.*
  Incline your ear to the voice of my <u>sup</u>-pli-*cation.*
  If you were to mark all iniquities,
    O God, <u>who</u> could *stand?*
  But there is forgiveness with you
    that you <u>may</u> be *worshiped.*

  I wait for the Lord, <u>my</u> soul *waits,*
  and in God's <u>word</u> I *hope;*
  My soul waits for the Lord
    more than those who watch <u>for</u> the *morning;*
  more than those who watch <u>for</u> the *morning.*

  O Israel, trust <u>in</u> the *Lord;*
    with God there is mercy and plen-<u>teous</u> re-*demption*
  for <u>the-</u> *Lord*
    will redeem Israel from <u>all</u> in-*iquities.*

(Psalm 130; alt DWV)

COLLECT
  O God whose Chosen One teaches true humility: Wash from us the
  stain of sin. Grant that, inspired by the example of Christ, we may
  serve at every time in every place. We pray through Jesus Christ, our
  Savior and brother. **Amen.**

[GLH]

[FOOTWASHING   (*During the footwashing, hymns may be sung*)

[EUCHARIST *(if not celebrated in another service on this day)*
    [*See "The Great Thanksgiving for Holy Thursday Evening,
        pages 64-65, UMBOW*]

COLLECT
    O Lover of souls, whose mercy is declared again and again in the Meal
    you instituted: So compose our hearts in yielding up this day to you,
    that our spirits may realize we have been reconciled to you. Awaking
    to the morning's light, help us know that we are bound anew in holy
    covenant with you in your cross and passion for the world. **Amen.**

    [DTB]

[THE LORD'S PRAYER *(if not prayed during Eucharist)*

[STRIPPING OF THE CHURCH *(in silence)*

[GOING FORTH IN SILENCE
[*Note: This office, along with others which follow, is not completed until the
Great Paschal Vigil. As a sign that we await the coming celebration of the
resurrection, these offices do not conclude in the usual way.*]

Jesus Washing the Disciples' Feet (from a 17th Century Armenian gospel)
©C. E. Visminas

Compline for Holy Thursday

(This office may be prayed immediately after Solemn Vespers)

CALL TO PRAYER

Let us go out to the Mount of Olives with Christ.
We will not desert you, O Lord.

NIGHT HYMN [77.77.77;Tune: REDHEAD 76, *UMH* 290]

Go to dark Gethsemane,
ye that feel the tempter's power;
your Redeemer's conflict see,
watch with him one bitter hour.
Turn not from his griefs away;
learn of Jesus Christ to pray.

See him at the judgment hall,
beaten, bound, reviled, arraigned;
O the wormwood and the gall!
O the pangs his soul sustained!
Shun not suffering, shame, or loss;
learn of Christ to bear the cross.

[JAMES MONTGOMERY, 1820, 1825, ALT.]

PRAYER OF CONFESSION

O good Shepherd, who laid down your life for the sheep,
remember us:
Lord, not our will, but yours be done.
O everlasting Power and Wisdom of the most high God, Word of God,
remember us:
Lord, not our will, but yours be done.
O Maker of the world, the Life of all, the Lord of angels,
remember us:
Lord, not our will, but yours be done.
O Lamb of God, who for us was led as a sheep to the slaughter,
remember us:
Lord, not our will, but yours be done.
O You who were seized, though guiltless, were buffeted, and given
over to robbers, remember us:
Lord, not our will, but yours be done.
You who alone by your death have overcome the death of our guilt,
remember us:
Lord, not our will, but yours be done.

[ADAPTED FROM MOZARABIC BREVIARY; TAR]

—*silence for confession*—

The saying is sure and worthy of full acceptance, that Christ Jesus came into the world to save sinners. If any one sins, we have an advocate with God, Jesus Christ the righteous; and he is the atoning sacrifice for our sins, and not for ours only but also for the sins of the whole world. In Christ, we are forgiven.
Thanks be to God.

(1 John 2:1b-2)

PSALTER
  Our help is in the name of the Lord;
  who made heaven and earth.

Psalm 80

> Hear us, Shepherd of Israel,
>   leader of <u>Jo</u>-seph's *flock.*
> From your throne on the cherubim
>   shine out for Ephraim,
>   for Benjamin <u>and</u> Ma-*nasseh.*
> Gather your strength,
>   <u>come -</u> , *save us!*
> Restore to us, God,
>   the light of your presence,
>   and we <u>shall</u> be *saved.*
>
> How long, Lord God of might,
>   will you smoulder with rage,
>   de-<u>spite</u> our *prayers?*
> For bread you feed us tears,
>   we drink them <u>by</u> the *barrel.*
> You let our neighbors mock,
>   our <u>ene</u>-mies *scorn us.*
> Restore to us, God of might,
>   the light of your presence,
>   and we <u>shall</u> be *saved.*
>
> You brought a vine from Egypt,
>   cleared out <u>nations</u> to *plant it;*
> you prepared the ground
>   and made it take root
>   to <u>fill</u> the *land.*
> It overshadowed the mountains,
>   towered over the <u>migh</u>-ty *cedars,*
> stretched its branches to the sea,
>   its roots to the <u>dis</u>-tant *river.*

Why have you now torn <u>down</u> its *walls?*
All who pass by <u>steal</u> the *grapes;*
Wild boars tear <u>up</u> its *roots,*
beasts de-<u>vour</u> its *fruit.*

Turn our way, God of might,
    look <u>down</u> from *heaven;*
tend this <u>vine</u> you *planted.*
Cherish <u>it</u> once *more.*
May those who slashed and burned it
    wither at <u>your</u> re-*buke.*

Rest your hand upon your chosen one
    who draws <u>strength</u> from *you.*
We have not <u>turned</u> from *you.*
Give us life again
    and we will in-<u>voke</u> your *name.*
Restore to us, Lord God of might,
    the light of your presence,
    and we <u>shall</u> be *saved.*

Glory to you, most blessed and <u>ho</u>-ly *Trinity,*
    One God, now and for-<u>ever.</u> A-*men.*

SCRIPTURE
    Year A: Mt. 26: 30-46
    Year B: Mk. 14: 26-42
    Year C: Lk. 22: 39-46

—silence—

(If Vespers, Compline and the Vigil are observed as a unit, omit the remainder of this office and proceed with the "Thanksgiving for the Light" in the Vigil)

PRAYERS
    THE KYRIE *(spoken)*
    Lord, have mercy upon us.
        Lord, have mercy upon us.
    Lord, have mercy upon us.

    Christ, have mercy upon us.
        Christ, have mercy upon us.
    Christ have mercy upon us.

    Lord, have mercy upon us.
        Lord, have mercy upon us.
    Lord, have mercy upon us.

COLLECT

Good Lord, give me the grace, in all my fear and agony, to have recourse to that great fear and agony that you, my Savior, had at the Mount of Olives before your most bitter passion, and as I meditate on it, may I receive comfort, consolation, and strength for my soul. **Amen.**

[ST. THOMAS MORE, 1474-1535]

[THE LORD'S PRAYER
(*if this office is not prayed in conjunction with Solemn Vespers and/or the Vigil*)

COMMENDATION

Guide us waking, O Lord, and guard us sleeping,
  that awake we may watch with Christ,
  and asleep we may rest in peace.
May the divine help remain with us always.
  And with those who are absent from us.

—silence—

Into your hands, O Lord, I commend my spirit,
  For you have redeemed me, O Lord,
  O God of Truth.

[ADAPTED FROM PSALM 4:8, THE SARUM BREVIARY, AND PSALM 30:5, TJC]

Let all depart in silence
or
remain for the Vigil

Vigil for Holy Thursday

[THE SERVICE OF LIGHT (*A candle is lit in silence unless the candle from Vespers is still burning. If Tenebrae is to be observed, seven additional candles may be lighted. If the Vigil is observed in conjunction with Vespers and Compline, the additional candles may be lighted at the beginning of Vespers.*)

THANKSGIVING FOR THE LIGHT
> On this, the night of your betrayal O Lord, your light flickered dimly in the garden. Although you were apprehended, we, your disciples, cannot comprehend the love with which your prayers were offered. Your light, O Lord, shines in the darkness of this world, yet we fear the overwhelming cloak of darkness which surrounds us this night. Illumine us, O Lord, that when those who are jealous of its splendor seek to conceal your light, you may shine ever more brightly through us. We pray to you, O God of light, through Jesus Christ our Lord. **Amen.**

[TAR]

—silence—

(the candle may be hidden under a container which will allow it to breathe and to be seen only dimly, symbolizing Christ's captivity)

THE SERVICE OF THE WORD

PRAYER FOR ILLUMINATION
> O Lord, we wait and watch with great anxiety and anticipation. Fill us with the light of your Spirit that we may hear again the story of our salvation. **Amen.**

[TAR]

THE LESSONS
> *(After the reading of each of the seven lessons, a time of silence is observed. The length of the silence should be determined by the desired length of the service. A candle may be extinguished after each reading.)*
> Isaiah 53:1-4
> Psalm 130 (*see p. 193 in Solemn Vespers above*; Canticle of Redemption)
> Hebrews 5:7-10

Year A:	Year B:	Year C:
Matthew. 26:47-56	Mark 14:43-52	Luke 22:47-53
Matthew 26:57-68	Mark 14:53-65	Luke 22:63-71

| Matthew 27:1-2, 11-14 | Mark 15:1-5 | Luke 23:1-5,13-16 |
| Matthew 27:15-26 | Mark 15:6-15 | Luke 23:18-25 |

CANTICLE 1 Peter 2:21-24

In Christ, our sins were crucified.
Through Christ, our injuries were healed.

Christ suffered for us
leaving us an example,
that we might walk
in his footsteps.

He did nothing wrong;
no false word
ever passed his lips.

When they cursed him
he returned no curse.
Tortured, he made no threats
but trusted in the perfect judge.

He carried our sins
in his body
to the cross,
that we might die to sin
and live for justice.
When he was wounded,
we were healed.

[ICEL]

PRAYER

Today, O good Jesus, for our sakes you did not hide your face from shame and spitting. Today, Jesus our Redeemer, for us you were mocked, struck by unbelievers and crowned with thorns. O good Jesus, you laid down your life on the cross for the sheep, and were crucified with robbers, and had nails driven through your hands and feet. Today, O good Jesus, put an end to our sins that on the day of resurrection we may be raised up to everlasting life. **Amen.**

[MOZARABIC SACRAMENTARY; ALT. TJC]

—silence—

CONCLUDING COLLECT

Be with us, merciful God, and protect us through the silent hours of this night, so that we, who are wearied by the changes and chances of this fleeting world, may rest upon your eternal changelessness; through Jesus Christ our Lord. **Amen.**   [BCP]

Depart in silence

Morning Prayer for Good Friday

CALL TO PRAYER

> Lord, we are ready to go with you to prison and death!
> **But you know that we will yet deny you.**

[HYMN [76.76.D; Tune: PASSION CHORALE, *UMH* 286]

> O sacred Head, now wounded,
> with grief and shame weighed down,
> now scornfully surrounded
> with thorns, thine only crown:
> how pale thou art with anguish,
> with sore abuse and scorn!
> How does that visage languish
> which once was bright as morn!
>
> What thou, my Lord, hast suffered
> was all for sinners' gain;
> Mine, mine was the transgression,
> but thine the deadly pain.
> Lo, here I fall, my Savior!
> 'Tis I deserve thy place;
> look on me with thy favor,
> vouchsafe to me thy grace.
>
> What language shall I borrow
> to thank thee, dearest friend,
> for this thy dying sorrow,
> thy pity without end?
> O make me thine forever,
> and should I fainting be,
> Lord, let me never, never
> outlive my love to thee.

[ANON. LATIN; TRANS. BY PAUL GERHARDT, 1656]

INVITATION

> Let us exalt our minds and kindle our hearts; let us not quench our
> spirits, but let us lay aside tiresome arguments and attach ourselves
> to the One on the cross. If it seems right, let us all go along with Peter
> to the house of Caiaphas, and with him, let us cry to Christ the words
> of Peter long ago— "Even if he goes to the cross and enters the tomb—
> we suffer with you, and we shall die with you and cry: 'Hasten, Holy
> One, save your sheep.'" **Amen.**

[Romanos, 6th C.]

I

Lord, ac-<u>cuse</u> my a-*ccusers,*
battle those who <u>bat</u>-tle *me.*
Take up <u>shield</u> and *buckler*
and rise to <u>my</u> *defense.*

Ready your axe and spear
  to cut <u>down</u> my *enemies.*
Tell me <u>you</u> will *save me.*
Punish those who <u>want</u> me *dead,*
make them retreat in disgrace,
  since they <u>seek</u> my *life.*

Let God's angel chase them
  as the wind <u>drives</u> the *chaff.*
Let God's angel pursue them
  down dark and <u>slip</u>-p'ry *paths.*
Without cause they <u>dug</u> a *pit,*
for no good reason
  <u>set</u> a *trap for me.*

Catch them off guard,
  snare them in their own trap.
  Let them <u>fall</u> to their *ruin.*
Then I will rejoice in the Lord
  and cele-<u>brate</u> God's *victory.*
From the marrow of my bones
  I will say: "Lord, <u>who</u> is *like you,*
rescuing the weak from the strong,
  the victim <u>from</u> the *robber."*

II

Witnesses <u>come -</u> *forward,*
  they accuse me falsely
  of things I <u>do</u> not *know.*
They repay me <u>evil</u> for *good,*
  leaving <u>me -</u> *desolate.*

When they were ill,
  I wore <u>sackcloth</u> and *fasted;*
now I take <u>back</u> my *prayer!*
I mourned for them
  as for my <u>brother</u> or *friend;*
I was weighed down with grief
  as if I had <u>lost</u> my *mother.*

But when I <u>stumbled</u>, they *cheered;*
they gathered to tear at me
　　and I did <u>not</u> know *why.*
They would not stop <u>their</u> at-*tack.*
The godless taunted me,
　　they clenched their <u>teeth</u> and *mocked.*

Lord, how long will <u>you</u> look *on?*
Save me from these roaring lions,
　　my <u>life</u> is *precious.*
Then I will thank you
　　when the as-<u>sem</u>-bly *gathers*
and praise you be-<u>fore</u> the *crowd.*

III

Give my lying enemies
　　no <u>chance</u> to *gloat,*
my reckless foes
　　no <u>chance</u> to *smirk.*
They do not speak peace
　　but devise schemes
　　to dis-<u>rupt</u> the *land.*
They laugh openly at me,
　　"See what <u>happened</u> to *you!"*

Lord, you <u>see</u> it *all!*
Do not keep silent,
　　do not <u>stand</u> a-*loof.*
Wake, rouse yourself in <u>my</u> de-*fense.*
Take up my cause, my <u>Lord</u> and *God.*

As you are just,
　　<u>judge</u> in my *favor.*
Do not give them <u>the</u> last *word.*
Do not let them think,
　　"Yes, we <u>got</u> our *way."*
Do not let them say,
　　"We <u>finished</u> you *off."*

When they delight in my ruin,
　　<u>bring them</u> dis-*grace.*
When they gloat at my expense,
　　<u>cover them</u> with *shame.*
But let my <u>friends</u> *rejoice*
when they <u>see me</u> a-*venged.*

Let them <u>shout</u> and say *always,*
"Great is the God who is pleased
   when a faithful <u>ser</u>-vant *triumphs.*"
Then I will tell <u>of</u> your *justice,*
sing your praises <u>all</u> day *long.*

SCRIPTURE   Year A: Matthew 26: 69-75
                  Year B: Mark 14: 66-72
                  Year C: Luke 22: 54-62

—silence—

CANTICLE OF ZECHARIAH (*spoken; see page 15*)

PRAYERS OF INTERCESSION AND SUPPLICATION
O most great and mighty God, enable us to do everything which you have commanded us, heartily, with good will and true love to your service.

Render us so mindful of the great love of our Lord that we may be zealously concerned for his glory and use our utmost diligence to commemorate his death and passion, making a joyful sacrifice of our souls and bodies to him, and earnestly desiring that his kingdom may come over all the earth.

Fulfill, most merciful Lord, all our petitions:
Especially, we pray for those who suffer . . .
   for those who struggle to remain faithful . . .
   for those who seek the courage of their convictions . . .
   for those who walk a lonely road . . .
   for your church, its ministry and mission . . .
   for our suffering world . . .

Help us not to deny you, O Lord Jesus, but to proclaim your name for ever. **Amen.**

[ADAPTED FROM JOHN WESLEY; TAR]

THE LORD'S PRAYER (*see p. 248*)
   (*See UMH 270-271 for musical settings*)

[HYMN [88.88.88;Tune: SELENA, *UMH* 287)
O Love divine, what hast thou done!
The immortal God hath died for me!
The Father's coeternal Son
bore all my sins upon the tree.
Th'immortal God for me hath died:
my Lord, my Love, is crucified!

Is crucified for me and you,
to bring us rebels back to God.
Believe, believe the record true,
ye all are bought with Jesus' blood.
Pardon for all flows from his side:
my Lord, my Love, is crucified!

Behold him, all ye that pass by,
the bleeding Prince of life and peace!
Come, sinners, see your Savior die,
and say, "Was ever grief like his?"
Come, feel with me his blood applied:
my Lord, my Love, is crucified!

[CHARLES WESLEY, 1742]

CONCLUDING PRAYER
O Lord, do not withhold your mercy;
let your steadfast love preserve me.

(Psalm 40: 11)

Depart in silence

Prayers of the Hours
of the Crucifixion
(prayed between noon and three on Good Friday)

GATHERING *in silence*

GREETING
Christ himself bore our sins in his body on the tree,
that we might die to sin and live to righteousness.
Blessed be the name of the Lord our God
who redeems us from sin and death.

COLLECT
Almighty God, graciously behold this your family, for whom our Lord
Jesus Christ was willing to be betrayed and given into the hands of
sinners, and to be lifted high upon the cross so that he might draw the
whole world to himself. Grant that we, who glory in his death for our
salvation, may also glory in his call to take up our cross and follow
him; through the same Jesus Christ our Lord. **Amen.**

[TRADITIONAL GOOD FRIDAY COLLECTS, ALT]

Sing, my tongue, the glorious battle,
sing the ending of the fray;
now above the cross, the trophy,
sound the loud triumphant lay:
tell how Christ, the world's Redeemer,
as a victim won the day.

Tell how, when at length the fullness
of th'appointed time was come,
Christ, the Word, was born of woman,
left for us his heavenly home;
showed us human life made perfect,
shone as light amid the gloom.

Thus, with thirty years accomplished,
went he forth from Nazareth,
destined, dedicated, willing,
wrought his work, and met his death.
Like a lamb he humbly yielded
on the cross his dying breath.

Faithful cross, thou sign of triumph,
now for us the noblest tree;
none in foliage, none in blossom,
none in fruit thy peer may be;
symbol of the world's redemption,
for the weight that hung on thee!

Unto God be praise and glory:
to the Father and the Son,
to th'eternal Spirit honor
now and evermore be done;
praise and glory in the highest,
while unending ages run.

[VENANTIUS HONORIUS FORTUNATUS, 6TH CENT.; TRANS. BY PERCY DEARMER, 1931]

LITANY OF CONFESSION AND PETITION

O Jesus, who did cleanse the lepers, heal the sick, and give sight to the blind, heal the diseases of our souls, open our eyes and fix them on our high calling, and cleanse our hearts from every desire which hinders the advancing of your glory.
Hear our prayer, O Lord.

O Jesus, poor and abject, unknown and despised, have mercy on us and let us not be ashamed to follow you.
  Hear our prayer, O Lord.
O Jesus, hated and persecuted, have mercy upon us and let us not be afraid to come after you.
  Hear our prayer, O Lord.
O Jesus, blasphemed, accused, and wrongfully condemned, have mercy upon us and teach us to endure the contradiction of sinners.
  Hear our prayer, O Lord.
O Jesus, clothed with a habit of reproach and shame, have mercy upon us and let us not seek our own glory.
  Hear our prayer, O Lord.
O Jesus, insulted, mocked, and spit upon, have mercy upon us and let us run with patience the race set before us.
  Hear our prayer, O Lord.
O Jesus, dragged to the pillar, scourged, and bathed in blood, have mercy upon us and let us not faint in the fiery trial.
  Hear our prayer, O Lord.
O Jesus, crowned with thorns and hailed in derision;
  Have mercy on us.
O Jesus, burdened with our sins and the curses of the people;
  Have mercy on us.
O Jesus, affronted, outraged, buffeted, overwhelmed with injuries, griefs, and humiliations;
  Have mercy on us.
O Jesus, hanging on the accursed tree, bowing the head, giving up the ghost, have mercy upon us and conform our souls and bodies to your holy, humble, suffering Spirit.
  Hear our prayer, O Lord. Amen.

[ADAPTED FROM JOHN WESLEY, PERSONAL PRAYERS, TAR]

OLD TESTAMENT LESSON Isaiah 52:13-53:12

PSALTER Psalm 22 (spoken)

I

Solo: God, my God,
            why have you abandoned me-
            far from my cry, my words of pain?
            I call by day, you do not answer;
            I call by night, but find no rest.

Choir 1:   You are the Holy One enthroned,
            the Praise of Israel.
            Our people trusted, they trusted you;
            you rescued them.

To you they cried, and they were saved;
they trusted and were not shamed.

Solo: But I am a worm, hardly human,
          despised by all, mocked by the crowd.
          All who see me jeer at me,
          sneer at me, shaking their heads:
          "You relied on God; let God help you!
          If God loves you, let God save you!"

Choir 2: But you, God, took me from the womb,
          you kept me safe at my mother's breast.
          I belonged to you from the time of birth,
          you are my God from my mother's womb.

Solo: Do not stay far off,
          danger is so close.
          I have no other help.
          Wild bulls surround me,
          bulls of Bashan encircle me,
          opening their jaws against me
          like roaring, ravening lions.

Choir 1: I am poured out like water,
          my bones are pulled apart,
          my heart is wax melting within me,
          my throat baked and dry,
          my tongue stuck to my jaws.
          You bring me down to the dust of death.

Solo: There are dogs all around me,
          a pack of villains corners me.
          They tear at my hands and feet,
          I can count all my bones.
          They stare at me and gloat.
          They take what I wore,
          they roll dice for my clothes.

Choir 2: Lord, do not stay far off,
          you, my strength, be quick to help.
          Save my neck from the sword,
          save my life from the dog's teeth,
          save me from the lion's jaws,
          save me from the bull's horns.

Unison: You hear me.

Solo: I will proclaim your name to my people,
I will praise you in the assembly.

Unison: Give praise, all who fear God:
revere and honor the Lord,
children of Israel, people of Jacob.
The Lord never scorns the afflicted,
never looks away, but hears their cry.

Choir 1: I will sing of you in the great assembly,
make good my promise before your faithful.
The poor shall eat all they want.
Seekers of God shall give praise.
"May your hearts live for ever!"

Choir 2: All peoples shall remember and turn,
all races will bow to the Lord,
who holds dominion over nations.
The well-fed crowd kneel before God,
all destined to die bow low.

Unison: My soul lives for the Lord!
My children will serve,
will proclaim God to the future,
announcing to peoples yet unborn,
"God saves."

THE GLORIA (*see back cover or:*)
  Glory to God, Love abounding be-<u>fore</u> all *ages;*
  Glory to God, Love shown forth in the self-emptying of <u>Je</u>-sus *Christ;*
  Glory to God, Love poured out through the <u>gift</u> of the *Spirit,*
    who fashions and renews the <u>face</u> of the *earth;*
  Glory to the holy and <u>bless</u>-ed *Trinity!*
  All things abiding in Love,
  Love abiding <u>in</u> all *things,*
  As it is now, <u>ev</u>-er *was,*
  And ever shall be for endless ages. <u>A</u>-*men.*

[DNP]

EPISTLE LESSON Hebrews 10:12-25

RESPONSORY
  Christ became obedient unto death, even death on a cross.
    Have mercy on us, Lord Jesus.

[The traditional readings for Good Friday come from the Gospel according to John (see UMBOW, p. 355 ff.) The service then continues with the Reproaches (see p. 214 below). The following readings, prayers and hymns based on the "words from the cross" provide an alternative.]

[WORDS FROM THE CROSS

Luke 23:32-38
"Father, forgive them; for they do not know what they are doing."

—silence—

Lord Jesus Christ, who forgave those who crucified you: teach us to forgive those who wrong us. Give us grace to confess our sin. May we receive your forgiveness with thankful hearts. Hear us, Holy Jesus. Amen.

[DWV]

[HYMN [87 87 D; Tune: PROMISE, *UMH* 707]
Here is love, vast as the ocean,
loving kindness as the flood,
when the Prince of life, our ransom,
shed for us his precious blood.
Who his love will not remember?
Who can cease to sing his praise?
He can never be forgotten
throughout heaven's eternal days.

On the mount of crucifixion
fountains opened deep and wide;
through the floodgates of God's mercy
flowed a vast and gracious tide.
Grace and love, like mighty rivers,
poured incessant from above,
and heav'ns peace and perfect justice
kissed a guilty world in love.

[ROBERT LOWRY 1826-99]

Luke 23:39-43
"Truly I tell you, today you will be with me in Paradise."

—silence—

Lord Jesus Christ, whose word to the thief fills us with hope: teach us to trust in you in life and death. Give us grace to receive your gift of eternal life so that even in suffering we may share your love. Hear us, Holy Jesus. Amen.

[DWV]

[RESPONSE: [Irr.; Tune: REMEMBER ME; *UMH* 488]
Jesus, remember me
when you come into your kingdom.
Jesus, remember me
When you come into your kingdom.

(Luke 23:42)

John 19:23-27
"Woman, here is your son." "Here is your mother."

—*silence*—

Lord Jesus Christ, who spoke words of care from the cross, teach us how to love those for whom we care. Release us from slavery to self so that we may enable others to be free. Give us all grace to serve you as we serve each other. Hear us, Holy Jesus. Amen.

[DWV]

[HYMN [887; Tune: STABAT MATER, *Hymnal* 1982, 159;
Voices United, 139]
At the cross her vigil keeping
stood the mournful mother weeping
where he hung, the dying Lord;
through her soul of joy bereaved,
bowed with sorrow, deeply grieved,
passed the sharp and piercing sword.

Who upon that mother gazing,
in her anguish so amazing,
born of woman, would not weep?
Who, of Christ's dear mother thinking
while her son that cup is drinking,
would not share her sorrow deep?

For his people's sins chastised
she beheld her Son despised,
scourged, and crowned with thorns entwined,
saw him then from judgment taken,
and in death by all forsaken,
till his spirit he resigned.

Near your cross, O Christ, abiding,
grief and love my heart dividing,
I with her would take my place:
by your saving cross uphold me,
in your dying, Christ, enfold me,
with the deathless arms of grace.

[JACOPONE DA TODI, 13TH C.; TRANS. EDWARD CASWALL (1814-1878)]

Mark 15:33-36
"My God, my God, why have you forsaken me?"

—*silence*—

Lord Jesus Christ, who knows our hours of anguish, teach us to be honest about our feelings. Give us grace to call out to you when we feel abandoned, with the assurance that your love never fails. Hear us, Holy Jesus. Amen.

[DWV]

[HYMN [76.76D Tune: PASSION CHORALE, *UMH* 286]
O Sacred Head, now wounded,
with grief and shame weighed down,
now scornfully surrounded
with thorns, thine only crown:
how pale thou art with anguish,
with sore abuse and scorn!
How does that visage languish
Which once was bright as morn!

What thou, my Lord, hast suffered
was all for sinners' gain;
Mine, mine was the transgression,
but thine the deadly pain.
Lo, here I fall, my Savior!
'Tis I deserve thy place;
look on me with thy favor,
vouchsafe to me thy grace.

What language shall I borrow
to thank thee, dearest friend,
for this thy dying sorrow,
thy pity without end?
O make me thine forever,
and should I fainting be,
Lord, let me never, never
outlive my love to thee.

[ANON, LATIN; TRANS. BY PAUL GERHARDT, 1656]

Matthew 27:39-43; John 19:28-29
"I am thirsty."

—*silence*—

Lord Jesus Christ, you cry to us that you are thirsty, yet we have nothing that will satisfy. Even though we have nothing of our own to offer, fill us with your living water that we may offer it to others in your name. Give us grace to yearn for a world in which the hungry are fed and the oppressed set free. Hear us, Holy Jesus. Amen.

[TAR; DWV]

[HYMN [88.88.88; Tune: SELENA, *UMH* 287]

O Love divine, what thou done!
The immortal God hath died for Me!
The Father's coeternal son
bore all my sins upon the tree.
Th'immortal God for me hath die:
my Lord, my Love, is crucified!

Is crucified for me and you,
to bring us rebels back to God.
Believe, believe the record true,
ye all are bought with Jesus' blood.
Pardon for all flows from his side:
my Lord, my Love, is crucified!

Behold him, all ye that pass by,
the bleeding Prince of life and peace!
Come, sinners, see your Savior die,
and say, "Was ever grief like his?"
Come, feel with me his blood applied:
my Lord, my Love, is crucified!

[CHARLES WESLEY, 1742]

Luke 23:44-46a
"Father, into your hands I commend my spirit."

—silence—

Lord Jesus Christ, who trusted in God in the face of death: teach us how to live and die as persons of faith. Give us grace to place ourselves in the hands of God, knowing that there is nothing in all creation which can separate us from your love. Hear us, Holy Jesus. Amen.

[DWV]

—silence—

[The Kyrie may be sung (see UMH 482). This is the last time music is used in the triduum until the Great Paschal Vigil of Easter.]

John 19:30-35
"It is finished."

—*silence*—

Lord Jesus Christ, who came to set us free: let the shadow of your cross fall upon us in this hour that we may wonder at the gift of your redeeming love, and be empowered by your Spirit to take up our own cross daily and follow you. Amen.

[BB]

Matthew 27:51-56

Meditation at the Cross

SILENT MEDITATION

THE REPROACHES:
CHRIST'S LAMENT AGAINST HIS FAITHLESS CHURCH

O my people, O my Church, what have I done to you, or in what have I offended you? I led you forth from the land of Egypt and delivered you by the waters of baptism, but you have prepared a cross for your Savior.

**R Holy God, holy and mighty,
holy and immortal One, have mercy upon us.**

—*silence*—

I led you through the desert forty years and fed you with manna; I brought you through times of persecution and of renewal and gave you my body, the bread of heaven; but you have prepared a cross for your Savior. **R**

—*silence*—

I made you branches of my vineyard and gave you the water of salvation, but when I was thirsty you gave me vinegar and gall and pierced with a spear the side of your Savior. **R**

—*silence*—

I went before you in a pillar of cloud, but you have led me to the judgment hall of Pilate. I brought you to a land of freedom and prosperity, but you have scourged, mocked, and beaten me. **R**

—*silence*—

I gave you a royal scepter, and bestowed the keys to the kingdom, but you have given me a crown of thorns. I raised you on high with great power, but you have hanged me on the cross. **R**

—silence—

My peace I gave, which the world cannot give, and washed your feet as a servant, but you draw the sword to strike in my name and seek high places in my kingdom. **R**

—silence—

I accepted the cup of suffering and death for your sakes, but you scatter and deny and abandon me. I sent the Spirit of truth to lead you, but you close your hearts to guidance. **R**

—silence—

I called you to go and bring forth fruit, but you cast lots for my clothing. I prayed that you all may be one, but you continue to quarrel and divide. **R**

—silence—

I grafted you into the tree of my chosen people Israel, but you turned on them with persecution and mass murder. I made you joint heirs with them of my covenants, but you made them scapegoats for your own guilt. **R**

—silence—

I came to you as the least of your brothers and sisters. I was hungry but you gave me no food, thirsty but you gave me no drink. I was a stranger but you did not welcome me, naked but you did not clothe me, sick and in prison but you did not visit me. **R**

SILENT MEDITATION
(*Persons may come and kneel before, or touch, the cross*)

THE LORD'S PRAYER (*spoken*)

Depart in silence

Evening Prayer for Good Friday

OPENING SENTENCES
O God, come to our assistance.
O Lord, hasten to help us.

PRAYER
Merciful God: Save us from hardness of heart! Help us receive the One who died for us so that we may repent, confess our sins, and be inspired to share your overflowing love; through Jesus Christ your Sacrifice. **Amen.**

[GLH]

PSALTER Psalm 4 (*spoken*)
Answer when I call, faithful God.
You cleared away my trouble;
be good to me,
listen to my prayer.

How long, proud fools,
will you insult my honor,
loving lies and chasing shadows?
Look! God astounds believers,
the Lord listens when I call.

Tremble, but do not despair.
Attend to your heart, be calm through the night,
worship with integrity,
trust in the Lord.

Cynics ask, "Who will bless us?
Even God has turned away."
You give my heart more joy
than all their grain and wine.
I sleep secure at night,
you keep me in your care.

SCRIPTURE   Year A: Matthew 27: 57-61
                Year B: Mark 15: 42-47
                Year C: Luke 23: 50-56

—silence—

LITANY

Joseph went to Pilate, pleaded with him and cried out:
   Give me that Stranger
who since his youth
has wandered as a stranger.
   Give me that Stranger
upon whom I look with wonder,
seeing him a guest of death.
   Give me that Stranger
whom envious ones
estrange from the world.
   Give me that Stranger
that I may bury him in a tomb,
who being a stranger has no place
whereupon to lay his head.
   Give me that Stranger
to whom his mother cried out
as she saw him dead:
"my Son, my senses are wounded
and my heart is burned
as I see you dead!
Yet, trusting in your resurrection,
I magnify you!"

In such words did the honorable Joseph plead with Pilate.
He took the Savior's body
  and, with fear, wrapped it in linen with spices.
And he placed you in a tomb.

[ORTHODOX LITURGY]

—silence—

PRAYERS OF INTERCESSION AND SUPPLICATION

Almighty God, you sent your Son into the world, not to condemn the world, but that the world through him might be saved; that all who believe in him might be delivered from the power of sin and death, and become heirs with him of everlasting life. We pray, therefore, for people everywhere according to their needs.

Let us pray for the holy catholic church of Christ throughout the world that God will confirm the church in faith, increase it in love and preserve it in peace.

—silence—

Let us pray for all nations and peoples of the earth, and for those in authority among them that by God's help they may seek justice and truth, and live in peace and concord.

—silence—

Let us pray for all who suffer and are afflicted in body or in mind that God in mercy will comfort and relieve them, and grant them the knowledge of God's love, and stir up in us the will and patience to minister to their needs.
—silence—

Let us pray for all who have not received the Gospel of Christ that God will open their hearts to the truth, and lead them to faith and obedience.
—silence—

O God, who for our redemption gave your only begotten Son to the death of the Cross, and has delivered us from the power of the enemy, grant us to die daily to sin, that we may evermore live with you, through the same Jesus Christ our Lord. **Amen.**

[ADAPTED FROM GREGORY THE GREAT AND BCP; TAR]

THE LORD'S PRAYER (*spoken; omit if the Vigil follows immediately*)

Depart in silence
or
remain for the Vigil

Vígíl
For Good Friday

[This office replaces both Compline and Mid-Night Matins; It may be prayed as an office, or used as the basis of an all-night vigil.]

OPENING SENTENCES
O God, come to our assistance.
O Lord hasten to help us.

COLLECT
Lord Jesus Christ, who this night rested in the tomb and so sanctified the grave to be a bed of hope to your people: make us deeply sorry for our sins so that when our days are earth are accomplished, we may live eternally with you; for with the Eternal Source of All and the Holy Spirit you live and reign, now and for ever. **Amen.**

[ANON]

SCRIPTURE Isaiah 53:5-12

—silence—

RESPONSORY   Lamentations 1:1-2; 2:18-19
How lonely she is now, the once crowded city!
Widowed is she who was mistress over nations;
The princess among the provinces has been made a toiling slave.
Bitterly she weeps at night, tears upon her cheeks,
With not one to console her of all her dear ones;
Her friends have all betrayed her and become her enemies.
Cry aloud to the Lord, O wall of daughter Zion!
Let tears stream down like a torrent day and night!
Give yourself no rest,
your eyes no respite!
Arise, cry out in the night, at the beginning of the watches!
Pour out your heart like water before the presence of the Lord!
Lift your hands to him for the lives of your children,
who faint for hunger at the head of every street.

PSALM 43 (*spoken in unison*)
Decide in my favor, God,
plead my case against the hateful,
defend me from liars and thugs.
For you are God my fortress.

Why have you forgotten me?
Why am I bent double
under the weight of enemies?

Send your light and truth.
They will escort me
to the holy mountain
where you make your home.

I will approach the altar of God,
God, my highest joy,
and praise you with the harp,
God, my God.

Why are you sad, my heart?
Why do you grieve?
Wait for the Lord.
I will yet praise God my savior.

—*silence*—

PSALM 44

I

Solo 1: We have heard the story
our ancestors told us
of your deeds so long ago:
how you, God, uprooted nations
to plant your own people,
how you weeded out others
so they could flourish.

Solo 2: Sword did not win the land,
might did not bring the victory;
it was your power, your light,
your love for them.
You, my God and King,
led Jacob to victory.
By the power of your name
we defeated our enemies,
crushing those who rose against us.

Choir 1: I did not rely on my bow,
my sword did not save me.
You, God, rescued us from danger
and put our foes to shame.
Every day we praise your name,
we never fail to thank you.

Choir 2:	Yet you scorn and demean us,
	no longer march at our side.
	You force us to retreat
	while the enemy plunders our goods.

You make us sheep for the slaughter,
scatter us among the nations.
You sell us for a pittance
and gain nothing in the bargain.

Choir 1: You reproach us before our neighbors;
they scoff and sneer,
making a joke of us,
shaking their heads.

Solo 1: Disgrace confronts me all day,
I turn red with shame
when I hear cruel taunts
from foes wanting revenge.

III

Choir 2: We endured all this,
though we did not forget you
or betray your covenant.
We have not turned from you
or wavered from your path.
Yet you banished us to the wilderness
where darkness overwhelms us.

Choir 1: If we should forget your name
and raise a prayer to foreign gods,
would you not find it out?
You know the secrets of the heart.
Still we are killed for your sake,
treated like sheep for slaughter.

IV

Solo 1: Wake up! Why do you sleep, Lord?
Wake up! Do not reject us for ever!
Why do you hide from us?
Why ignore how much we suffer?

Solo 2: We grovel in the dust,
clutching at the ground.
Wake up and help us.
Rescue us! Your love demands it.

—*silence*—

PSALM 55

I

Solo 1:   Listen, God, to my plea,
do not ignore my cry.
Listen and answer,
I shake with grief
at the furor of my enemies.
They threaten and attack me;
they shout out curses,
venting their anger against me.

Solo 2:   My heart is pounding,
I can feel the touch of death.
Terror holds me in its grip,
trembling seizes me.

Unison: "If I had wings like a dove,
I would fly far and rest,
fly far away to the wilds
to escape the raging storm."

Solo 1:   Confuse their speech, Lord!
I see violence and strife
stalk their city walls
both day and night.
Evil and destruction
live in their midst;
oppression and deceit
never leave the public square.

Solo 2:   If my enemy insults me,
I can bear it;
if a foe rises against me,
I can hide myself.
But it was you, my own friend,
the one I knew so well.
With you I could always talk,
even as we walked to the temple,
my companion amid the crowd.

II

Solo 1:   Death to them all!
Let them fall into Sheol alive,
for evil fills their homes
and lives among them.

Solo 2:	I call out to God who rescues me. Morning, noon, and night I plead my case.
Solo 1:	God hears my cry, brings me to safety when the battle is raging and my foes are many. Enthroned for ever, God acts by humbling them because they refuse to change; they will not fear God.
Solo 2:	My friend turned traitor and broke old promises, spoke words smooth as butter while intending war, words that flowed like oil but cut like a sword.
Unison:	Give your burden to the Lord, who will be your support. If you are faithful, God will not let you fall.

III

Solo 1:	O God, hurl the bloodthirsty into the pit of destruction. Let traitors live only half their days.
Unison:	But as for me, I trust in you.

—*silence*—

PSALM 80

I

Choir 1:	Hear us, Shepherd of Israel, leader of Joseph's flock. From your throne on the cherubim shine out for Ephraim, for Benjamin and Manasseh. Gather your strength, come, save us!

Restore to us, God,
the light of your presence,
and we shall be saved.

II

Choir 2: How long, Lord God of might,
will you smoulder with rage,
despite our prayers?
For bread you feed us tears,
we drink them by the barrel.
You let our neighbors mock,
our enemies scorn us.
Restore to us, God of might,
the light of your presence,
and we shall be saved.

III

Choir 1: You brought a vine from Egypt,
cleared out nations to plant it;
you prepared the ground
and made it take root
to fill the land.
It overshadowed the mountains,
towered over the mighty cedars,
stretched its branches to the sea,
its roots to the distant river.

Choir 2: Why have you now torn down its walls?
All who pass by steal the grapes;
Wild boars tear up its roots,
beasts devour its fruit.
Turn our way, God of might,
look down from heaven;
tend this vine you planted.
Cherish it once more.
May those who slashed and burned it
wither at your rebuke.

IV

Unison: Rest your hand upon your chosen one
who draws strength from you.
We have not turned from you.
Give us life again
and we will invoke your name.
Restore to us, Lord God of might,
the light of your presence,
and we shall be saved.

—silence—

EPISTLE Hebrews 4:14-16

GOSPEL LESSON   Year A: Matthew 24:36-44
                    Year B: Mark 13:32-37
                    Year C: Luke 21:34-36

—silence—

LITANY OF PETITION
  Soul of Christ,
    be my sanctification;
  Body of Christ,
    be my salvation;
  Blood of Christ,
    fill all my veins;
  Water of Christ's side,
    wash out my stains;
  Passion of Christ,
    my comfort be;
  O good Jesus,
    listen to me:
  In your wounds I fain would hide,
    ne'er to be parted from your side;
  Guard me, should the foes assail me;
    call me when my life shall fail me,
  Bid me come to you above,
    with your saints to sing your love,
    world without end. Amen.

[ANIMA CHRISTI, 14TH C. TR. JOHN HENRY NEWMAN, 1801-90]

THE KYRIE (*spoken*)
  Lord, have mercy upon us.
    Christ have mercy upon us.
  Lord, have mercy upon us.

COMMENDATION
  In peace we will lie down and sleep.
    In the Lord alone we safely rest.
  Guide us waking, O Lord, and guard us sleeping,
    that awake we may watch with Christ,
    and asleep we may rest in peace.
  May the divine help remain with us always.
    And with those who are absent from us.

—silence—

Into your hands, O Lord, I commend my spirit,
For you have redeemed me, O Lord, O God of Truth.

CANTICLE OF SIMEON (*spoken only*)
Lord, you have now set your servant free
to go in peace as you have promised;
for these eyes of mine have seen the Savior,
Whom you have prepared for all the world to see.
A Light to enlighten the nations,
And the glory of your people Israel.

—silence—

COLLECT
O Lord, my God, we sing to you a burial song and a funeral chant,
who by your entombment has opened for us a door to life, and by
your dying has brought an end to our death and hell. In sleep we lie
down with you to rise to morning's light. Grant us a peaceful rest and
a perfect end. **Amen.**

[ADAPTED FROM HOLY SATURDAY ORTHODOX LITURGY; DTB]

THE LORD'S PRAYER (*spoken*)

Depart in silence

Morning Prayer for Holy Saturday
(The Great Sabbath)

OPENING SENTENCES

Out of the depths I cry to you, O LORD.
Lord, hear my voice!
Come, faithful, come, let us keep watch beside Christ's tomb,
He who gives life to those who live among the tombs.
Come, let us cry out with the voice of the psalmist:
What profit is there in death?
Will the dust praise you?
Will it tell of your faithfulness?
Weeping may tarry for the night, but joy comes in the morning.
"Arise, O Lord! Let not mortals prevail,
Lift up your hand; forget not the afflicted."

[Adapted from Holy Saturday Orthodox liturgy; TAR]
(Psalm 30:9; 9:19, 10:12)

MORNING COLLECT

Almighty and everlasting God, the comfort of the sad, the strength of sufferers, let the prayers of those that cry out of any tribulation come unto you, that all may rejoice to find that your mercy is present with them in their afflictions; through Jesus Christ our Lord. **Amen.**

[Gelasian Sacramentary, 5th c.]

PSALTER   Psalm 130

Choir 1:   From the depths I call to you,
Lord, hear my cry.
Catch the sound of my voice
raised up, pleading.

Choir 2:   If you record our sins,
Lord, who could survive?
But because you forgive
we stand in awe.
I trust in God's word,
I trust in the Lord.
More than sentries for dawn
I watch for the Lord.

Unison: More than sentries for dawn let Israel watch.
The Lord will bring mercy
and grant full pardon.
The Lord will free Israel
from all its sins.

SCRIPTURE Matthew 27: 62-66

CANTICLE OF ZECHARIAH (*see page 15, spoken only*)

PRAYERS OF INTERCESSION AND SUPPLICATION
Creator and Architect of earth and all stars, cause us to rest from our labors on this holy sabbath as you rested from your work. Cause us to anticipate the rest that comes in death as we remember Jesus in the tomb; the rest that comes to those who are spent, exhausted, inert. Cause us to wait in hope for the break of day and the resurrection.
Remember those who have died and those who mourn their death . . .
Remember those who died through violence and the miscarriage of justice . . .
Remember those who died confessing your name for the sake of the Gospel . . .
Remember those who resist trusting you in life and in death . . .
Remember those who cannot rest . . .
And remember us in our restless thoughts, strivings, and failures . . .
[DTB]

COLLECT
O ruler of the ages, through your passion you fulfilled the plan of salvation. As you keep Sabbath in the tomb, you grant us a new Sabbath. Unto you we cry aloud: Arise, O Lord, judge the earth, for measureless is your great mercy, reigning for ever. Amen.
[ADAPTED FROM ORTHODOX HOLY SATURDAY MATINS; TAR]

THE LORD'S PRAYER (*spoken*)
(*See p. 248*)

Depart in silence

Mid-Morning Prayer
for Holy Saturday

OPENING SENTENCES
    Out of the depths I cry to you, O LORD.
      Lord, hear my voice!

PRAYER
    Jesus my Lord,
    Come to me, comfort me, console me.
    Visit the hearts in strange lands yearning for you.
    Visit the dying and those who have died without you.
    Jesus, my Lord,
    Visit also those who persecute you.
    Lord Jesus, you are my light in the darkness.
    You are my warmth in the cold.
    You are my happiness in sorrow.

[ANONYMOUS]

PSALTER Psalm 42:1-6a

Choir 1:   As a deer craves running water,
               I thirst for you, my God;
               I thirst for God,
               the living God.

Choir 2:   When will I see your face?
               Tears are my steady diet.
               Day and night I hear,
               "Where is your God?"

Choir 1:   I cry my heart out,
               I remember better days:
               when I entered the house of God,
               I was caught in the joyful sound
               of pilgrims giving thanks.

Choir 2:   Why are you sad, my heart?
               Why do you grieve?
               Wait for the Lord.
               I will yet praise God my savior.

SCRIPTURE Job 14:1-14

—silence—

RESPONSORY: (in unison)
> Let the same mind be in you that was in Christ Jesus,
>> who, though he was in the form of God,
>>> did not regard equality with God
>>> as something to be exploited,
>> but emptied himself,
>>> taking the form of a slave,
>>> being born in human likeness.
>> And being found in human form,
>>> he humbled himself
>>> and became obedient to the point of death—
>> even death on a cross.

(Philippians 2: 5-8)

[SILENT PRAYER]

COLLECT
> O Lord, who washes out all our offenses, comfort us who faithfully call upon you; blot out our transgressions, and restore us from death to the land of the living; through Christ our Lord. **Amen.**

[Sᴀʀᴜᴍ Bʀᴇᴠɪᴀʀʏ, 11ᴛʜ ᴄ.]

THE LORD'S PRAYER (*spoken*)

Depart in silence

Mid-Day Prayer
for Holy Saturday

OPENING SENTENCES
> Out of the depths I cry to you, O LORD.
> **Lord, hear my voice!**

PRAYER
> O God, by the suffering of Christ your Son you have saved us from death. We bear the likeness of sinful humanity. May the sanctifying power of grace help us to put on the likeness of Jesus Christ. In your goodness raise up your faithful people buried with him in baptism, to be one with him in your love. **Amen.**

[ᴀᴅᴀᴘᴛᴇᴅ Rᴏᴍᴀɴ Rɪᴛᴇ & Rᴏᴍᴀɴ Lɪᴛᴜʀɢʏ ᴏꜰ ᴛʜᴇ Hᴏᴜʀs; TAR; DWV]

PSALTER: Psalm 42: 6b-11

Solo 1:   My heart is sad.
              Even from Jordan and Hermon,
              from the peak of Mizar,
              I remember you.
              There the deep roars to deep;
              your torrents crash over me.
              The love God summoned by day
              sustained my praise by night,
              my prayer to the living God.

Solo 2:   I complain to God,
              who I thought was rock:
              "Why have you forgotten me?
              Why am I bent double
              under the weight of enemies
              "Their insults grind me to dust.

Unison: Day and night they say,
              'Where is your God?'"
              Why are you sad, my heart?
              Why do you grieve?
              Wait for the Lord.
              I will yet praise God my savior.

THE KYRIE   (*spoken*)
   Lord, have mercy.
      Lord, have mercy.
   Lord, have mercy.

   Christ, have mercy.
      Christ, have mercy.
   Christ, have mercy.

   Lord, have mercy.
      Lord, have mercy.
   Lord, have mercy.

SCRIPTURE Jeremiah 20: 7-12

—silence—

RESPONSORY

We know that the whole creation has been groaning in labor pains until now;

and not only the creation, but we ourselves, who have the first fruits of the Spirit, groan inwardly while we wait for adoption, the redemption of our bodies.

For in hope we were saved.

Now hope that is seen is not hope. For who hopes for what is seen? But if we hope for what we do not see, we wait for it with patience.

(Romans 8:22-25)

[SILENT PRAYER

COLLECT

Gracious God, keep us this day in your fear and favor, and teach us in all our thoughts, words, and works to live to your glory. If you guide us not, we go astray; if you uphold us not, we fall. Let your good providence be our defense and your good Spirit our guide and counselor, and supporter in all our ways. And grant that we may do always what is acceptable in your sight, through Jesus Christ our Lord, in whose holy name we lift up these our imperfect prayers: Our Father...

[JOHN WESLEY]

THE LORD'S PRAYER (*spoken*)

(*see p. 248*)

Depart in silence

Mið-Afternoon Prayer for Holy Saturday

OPENING SENTENCES

Out of the depths I cry to you, O LORD.

Lord, hear my voice!

PRAYER

O Merciful God, who answers the poor,

Answer us.

O Merciful God, who answers the lowly in spirit,

Answer us.

O Merciful God, who answers the broken of heart,
  Answer us.
O Merciful God,
  Answer us.
O Merciful God,
  Have compassion.
O Merciful God,
  Redeem.
O Merciful God,
  Save.
O Merciful God, have pity upon us,
  Now,
  Speedily,
  And at a near time. Amen.

[JEWISH PRAYER ON DAY OF ATONEMENT]

PSALTER   Psalm 31: 9-16

Solo 1:   Pity me, Lord,
          I hurt all over;
          my eyes are swollen,
          my heart and body ache.
          Grief consumes my life,
          sighs fill my days;
          guilt saps my strength,
          my bones dissolve.

Solo 2:   Enemies mock me,
          make me the butt of jokes.
          Neighbors scorn me,
          strangers avoid me.
          Forgotten like the dead,
          I am a shattered jar.
          I hear the crowd whisper,
          "Attack on every side!"
          as they scheme to take my life.

Choir 1:   But I trust in you, Lord.
          I say, "You are my God,
          my life is in your hands."
          Snatch me from the enemy,
          ruthless in their chase.

Choir 2:   Look on me with love,
          save your servant.

I call on you;
save me from shame!

Solo 1:   Shame the guilty,
            silence them with the grave.

SCRIPTURE Isaiah 51:9-11

—silence—

RESPONSORY:
Set your minds on things that are above, not on things that are on earth, for you have died, and your life is hidden with Christ in God. When Christ who is your life is revealed, then you also will be revealed with him in glory.

(Colossians 3: 2-4)

[SILENT PRAYER]

COLLECT
Most merciful God, the helper of all, so strengthen us by your power that our sorrow may be turned into joy, and we may continually glorify your holy name; through Jesus Christ our Lord. **Amen.**

[SARUM BREVIARY, 11TH C.]

THE LORD'S PRAYER *(spoken)*
    (see p. 248)

Depart in silence

The Great Paschal Vígil

The First Service of Easter

[This, the most holy and joyful festival of the Christian year, celebrates the whole story of salvation history culminating in the paschal mystery of Christ's death and resurrection. Through Light, Word, Water, and Feast we experience anew our pass-over from bondage to freedom, from death to life. This service should be a "people's office" open to the whole congregation. Only when circumstances make that impossible or unwise should this office be prayed apart from the congregation. Even then, it is prayed in concert with Christians of all times and places, whether dispersed or gathered.]

THE SERVICE OF LIGHT

GATHERING *in silence as a new fire is kindled*

GREETING AND INTRODUCTION
> Dear friends in Christ, on this most holy night, when our Lord Jesus Christ passed from death to life, we gather as the Church to watch and pray. We will celebrate Christ's baptism and his holy resurrection which gives us life and salvation. This is the passover of Christ, in which, by hearing his Word and celebrating his Sacraments, we share in his victory over death.
>
> [ADAPT FROM BCP & 4TH C. PRAYER; TAR]

OPENING PRAYER
> O Savior Jesus Christ, grant light to our minds and hearts. Enlighten us as you enlightened the women who came to your tomb with spices, so they could anoint your body, the source of life. Since you have raised us up and delivered us from the darkness of sin and death, give us grace through your loving kindness that we may kindle our lamps with the light of your radiant and glorious resurrection. **Amen.**
>
> [ADAPTED FROM ORTHODOX LITURGY; TAR; DWV]

LIGHTING OF THE PASCHAL CANDLE
Hear the Word of God:

> In the beginning was the Word and the Word was with God and the Word was God. . . . In him was life, and the life was the light of all. The light shines in the darkness and the darkness has not overcome it.
>
> (John 1:1, 4-5)

PROCESSION

[if there is a congregational candlelight procession, the following invitation may be issued:]

Come, O Faithful, and take light from the Light that never fades;
  come and glorify Christ who is risen from the dead!
Christ is risen from the dead!
He has crushed death by his death
  and bestowed life upon those who lay in the tomb.

[ORTHODOX LITURGY]

(During the procession the leader pauses three times and the following litany is sung)

EXSULTET
  [The Exsultet may be spoken, chanted, or sung to an improvised melody.]

R:

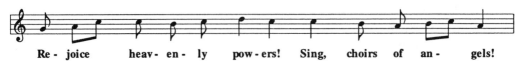

Rejoice, heavenly powers! Sing, <u>choirs</u> of *angels!*
Exult, all creation 'round God's *throne!*
Jesus Christ, our <u>King,</u> is *risen!*
Sound the trumpet <u>of</u> sal-*vation!*   **R**

Rejoice, O earth, in <u>shin</u>-ing *splendor,*
radiant in the brightness <u>of</u> our *King!*
Christ has conquered! <u>Glo</u>-ry *fills you!*
Darkness <u>vanishes</u> for *ever!*   **R**

Rejoice, O holy Church! Ex-<u>ult</u> in *glory!*
The risen Savior <u>shines</u> u-*pon you!*
Let this place re-<u>sound</u> with *joy,*
echoing the mighty song of <u>all</u> God's *people!*   **R**

It is truly right that <u>we</u> should *praise you,*
invisible, almighty, and eternal God,
  and your Son, <u>Je</u>-sus *Christ.*
For Christ has ransomed us <u>with</u> his *blood,*
and paid the debt of Adam's sin
  to deliver your <u>faith</u>-ful *people!*   R

This is our Passover feast,
  when Christ, the true <u>Lamb,</u> is *slain.*
This is the night when first you <u>saved</u> our *forbears.*
You freed the people of Israel <u>from</u> their *slavery*
and led them with dry feet <u>through</u> the *sea.*   R

This is the night when the pillar of fire destroyed the
  <u>darkness</u> of *sin!*
This is the night when Christians everywhere,
  washed clean of sin and freed from all defilement,
  are restored to grace and grow to-<u>gether</u> in *holiness.*
This is the night when Jesus Christ broke the chains of death
  and rose triumphant <u>from</u> the *grave.*
Night truly blessed, when heaven is wedded to earth,
  and we are recon-<u>ciled</u> to *you!*   R

Accept this Easter candle, a flame divided <u>but</u> un-*dimmed,*
a pillar of fire that glows <u>to</u> your *honor.*
Let it mingle with the <u>lights</u> of *heaven,*
and continue bravely burning
  to dispel the darkness <u>of</u> the *night!*   R

May the Morning Star, which never sets,
  find this <u>flame</u> still *burning.*
Christ, that Morning Star, who came back <u>from</u> the *dead,*
who shed his peaceful light on <u>all</u> cre-*ation,*
your Son who lives and reigns for <u>ever</u> and *ever.*   R

[UMBOW]

THE SERVICE OF THE WORD

INTRODUCTION
Let us hear the record of God's saving deeds and pray that our God
will bring each of us to the fullness of redemption.

[BCP]

THE CREATION
Genesis 1:1-2:4a

—silence—

O God, who wonderfully created, and yet more wonderfully restored, the dignity of human nature: Grant that we may share the divine life of him who humbled himself to share our humanity, your Son Jesus Christ our Lord. **Amen.**

[BCP]

HYMN [Tune: LACQUIPARLE, Irr., *UMH* 148]

Many and great, O God, are thy things,
maker of earth and sky.
Thy hands have set the heavens with stars
thy fingers spread the mountains and plains.
Lo, at they word the waters were formed;
deep seas obey thy voice.

Grant unto us communion with thee,
thou star abiding one;
come unto us and dwell with us;
with thee are found the gifts of life.
Bless us with life that has no end,
eternal life with thee.

[JOSEPH R. RENVILLE, CA. 1846]

THE FLOOD
Genesis 7:1-5, 11-18; 8:6-18; 9:8-13

—*silence*—

Almighty God of heaven and earth, you set in the clouds a rainbow to be a sign of your covenant with all living things: Grant that we, who are saved through water and the Spirit, may know again the mark of your covenant with us in baptism through Jesus Christ our Lord. **Amen.**

[BCP alt TAR]

HYMN [77.77 D; Tune: ABERYSTWYTH, *UMH* 479]

Jesus, lover of my soul,
let me to thy bosom fly,
while the nearer waters roll,
while the tempest still is high.
Hide me, O my Savior, hide,
till the storm of life is past;
safe into the haven guide;
O receive my soul at last

Other refuge have I none,
hangs my helpless soul on thee;
leave, ah! leave me not alone,
still support and comfort me.

All my trust on thee is stayed,
all my help from thee I bring;
cover my defenseless head
with the shadow of thy wing.

[CHARLES WESLEY, 1740]

ABRAHAM'S TRUST IN GOD
Genesis 22: 1-18

—silence—

Gracious God of all believers, through Abraham's trust in your promise you made known your faithful love to countless numbers. By the grace of Christ's sacrifice fulfill in your Church and in all creation the joy of your promise and new covenant. **Amen.**

[UMBOW]

HYMN [66.84 D; Tune: LEONI, *UMH* 116, stanza 1)
The God of Abraham praise, who reigns enthroned above;
Ancient of Everlasting Days, and God of love;
Jehovah, great I AM! by earth and heaven confessed;
I bow and bless the sacred name for ever blest.

[DANIEL BEN JUDAH, CA. 1400]

ISRAEL'S DELIVERANCE AT THE RED SEA
Exodus 14:10-31

—silence—

Lord God, in the new covenant you shed light on the miracles you worked in ancient times: the Red Sea is a symbol of our baptism, and the nation you freed from slavery is a sign of your Christian people. May every nation share the faith and privilege of Israel and come to new birth in the Holy Spirit. **Amen.**

[ROMAN RITE]

HYMN [76.76.D; Tune: ST. KEVIN, *UMH* 315, stanza 1]
Come, ye faithful, raise the strain
of triumphant gladness;
God hath brought forth Israel
into joy from sadness;
loosed from Pharaoh's bitter yoke
Jacob's sons and daughters,
led them with unmoistened foot
through the Red Sea waters.

[JOHN OF DAMASCUS; TRANS. BY JOHN MASON NEALE, 1859]

SALVATION OFFERED FREELY TO ALL
Isaiah 55: 1-5

—silence—

Creator of all things, you freely offer water to the thirsty and food to
the hungry. Refresh us by the water of baptism and feed us with the
bread and wine of your table, that your Word may bear fruit in our
lives, and bring us all to your heavenly banquet; through Jesus Christ
our Lord. **Amen.**   [UMBOW]

HYMN [87.87.87; Tune: CWM RHONDDA, *UMH* 127]
Guide me, O thou great Redeemer,
pilgrim through this barren land.
I am weak, but thou art mighty;
hold me with thy powerful hand.
Bread of heaven, bread of heaven,
feed me till I want no more; (want no more)
feed me till I want no more.

Open now the crystal fountain,
whence the healing stream doth flow;
let the fire and cloudy pillar
lead me all my journey through.
Strong deliverer, strong deliverer,
be thou still my strength and shield; (strength and shield)
by thou still my strength and shield.
[WILLIAM WILLIAMS, 1745; ALT.]

A NEW HEART AND A NEW SPIRIT
Ezekiel 36: 24-28

—silence—

God of unchanging power and light, look with mercy and favor on
your entire church. Bring lasting salvation to humankind, so that the
world may see the fallen lifted up, the old made new, and all things
brought to perfection, through him who is their origin, our Lord Jesus
Christ. **Amen.**

[ROMAN RITE]

RESPONSE [SM; Tune: TRENTHAM, (*UMH* 420)]
Breathe on me, Breath of God,
fill me with life anew,
that I may love what thou dost love,
and do what thou wouldst do.

Breathe on me, Breath of God,
Till I am wholly thine,
Till all this earthly part of me
Glows with thy fire divine.

[Edwin Hatch, 1878 (John 20:22)]

NEW LIFE FOR GOD'S PEOPLE
Ezekiel 37: 1-14

—silence—

Psalm 143

I

Hear me, <u>faith</u>-ful *Lord!*
bend to my prayer, <u>show</u> com-*passion.*
Do not <u>judge</u> me *harshly;*
in your sight, <u>no one</u> is *just.*

II

My enemy hunts me down, <u>grinding me</u> to *dust,*
caging me with the dead in <u>last</u>-ing *darkness.*
My strength <u>drains</u> a-*way,*
my <u>heart</u> is *numb.*

I remember the <u>an</u>-cient *days,*
I recall your wonders, the <u>work</u> of your *hands.*
Dry as <u>thir</u>-sty *land,*
I reach <u>out</u> for *you.*

III

Answer me <u>quick</u>-ly, *Lord.*
My <u>strength</u> is *spent.*
Do not <u>hide</u> from *me*
or I will fall <u>into</u> the *grave.*

Let morning announce your love, for it is <u>you</u> I *trust.*
Show me the right way, I offer <u>you</u> my-*self.*
Rescue me from my foes, you are my only <u>ref</u>-uge, *Lord.*
Teach me your will, for <u>you are</u> my *God.*

Graciously lead me, Lord, on to <u>lev</u>-el *ground.*
I call on your just name, keep me safe, <u>free</u> from *danger.*
In your great love for me, dis-<u>arm</u> my *enemies,*
destroy their power, for I be-<u>long</u> to *you.*

Eternal God, you raised from the dead our Lord Jesus and by your Holy Spirit brought to life your Church. Breathe upon us again with your spirit and give new life to your people, through the same Jesus Christ our Redeemer. **Amen.**

[UMBOW]

HYMN [SM; Tune: ST. MICHAEL, *UMH* 388, stanzas 1, 2]

O come and dwell in me,
Spirit of power within,
and bring the glorious liberty
from sorrow, fear, and sin.

Hasten the joyful day
which shall my sins consume,
when old things shall be done away,
and all things new become.

[CHARLES WESLEY, 1762]

BURIED AND RAISED WITH CHRIST IN BAPTISM
Romans 6: 3-11

—*silence*—

Let us chant Alleluia. Then the word of scripture will be accomplished, the word not of combatants any more, but of victors;
   Death has been swallowed up in victory.
Let us chant Alleluia.
   O Death, where is your sting?

O Blessed Alleluia of heaven! No more anguish, no more adversity. No more enemy. No more love of destruction. Up above, praise to God, and here below, praise to God. Praise mingled with fear here, but without disturbance above. Here the one who chants must die, but there will we live for ever; here we chant in hope, there, in possession, here it is Alleluia on the way, there it is Alleluia on arriving home. Let us chant Alleluia!

[AUGUSTINE, 5TH C.]

THE ALLELUIA [*UMH* 306; Antiphon only]
   Alleluia! Alleluia! Alleluia!

GOSPEL LESSON John 20: 1-18

HYMN [76.76D; Tune: LANCASHIRE, *UMH* 303]

The day of resurrection!
Earth, tell it out abroad;

the passover of gladness,
the passover of God.
From death to life eternal,
from earth unto the sky,
our Christ hath brought us over,
with hymns of victory.

Our hearts be pure from evil,
that we may see aright
the Lord in rays eternal
of resurrection light;
and listening to his accents,
may hear, so calm and plain,
his own "All hail!" and hearing,
may raise the victor strain.

Now let the heavens be joyful!
Let earth the song begin!
Let the round world keep triumph,
and all that is therein!
Let all things seen and unseen
their notes in gladness blend,
for Christ the Lord hath risen,
our joy that hath no end.

[JOHN OF DAMASCUS; TRANS. BY JOHN MASON NEALE, 1862]

RESPONSORY

O death, where is your sting? O Grave, where is your victory? Christ
is risen and you are abolished, Christ is risen and the demons are cast
down, Christ is risen and the angels rejoice, Christ is risen and life is
freed, Christ is risen and the tomb is emptied of the dead:
**Christ, being risen from the dead, has become the Leader
and Reviver of those who had fallen asleep. To him be glory and
power for ever and ever. Amen!**

[JOHN CHRYSOSTOM, 5TH C.]

HOMILY

THE SERVICE OF WATER

HYMN [10 10 10 with Alleluias; Tune: ENGELBERG, *UMH* 610]
We know that Christ is raised and dies no more.
Embraced by death, he broke its fearful hold,
and our despair he turned to blazing joy.
Alleluia!

We share by water in his saving death.
Reborn, we share with him an Easter life
as living members of a living Christ.
Alleluia!

A new creation comes to life and grows
as Christ's new body takes on flesh and blood.
The universe restored and whole will sing:
Alleluia!

[JOHN BROWNLOW GEYER, 1969 (ROM. 6:3-11)]

INVITATION TO THE BAPTISMAL COVENANT

Brothers and sisters in Christ, we are bound together in the communion of all the saints by our baptism, through which we are initiated into Christ's holy church, dying and rising with Christ through God's grace. Therefore, let us come with faith in the company of the whole body of Christ.

LITANY OF THE SAINTS

Mary, blessed mother of our Lord,
   R: Stand beside us.
Peter and Andrew, James, and John,
   disciples of our Lord, **R**
Mary Magdalene, Matthew, Mark, Luke and John,
   proclaimers of good news, **R**
Polycarp, Agnes, and Justin,
   martyrs and confessors, **R**
Athanasius, Augustine, and Basil,
   theologians of the faith, **R**
Luther and Calvin, Zwingli and Hus,
   reformers of the church, **R**
Francis and Clare, Benedict and Scholastica,
   seekers of the holy life, **R**
The Wesleys: Susanna, John and Charles,
   witnesses of grace, **R**
Victims of lynching, known and unknown,
   brothers and sisters of Stephen the martyr, **R**
Unnamed faithful ones in all times and places,
   baptized through death and life, **R**

THE BAPTISMAL COVENANT

(*see denominational resources, for example* UMH *pp. 33 or 50;
beginning after the introduction*)

THE SERVICE OF THE TABLE: THE EASTER FEAST

HYMN [77.79; Tune: CANTERBURY, *UMH* 465]
> At the Lamb's high feast we sing
> praise to our victorious King,
> who has washed us in the tide
> flowing from his pierced side.
>
> Praise we Christ, whose blood was shed,
> paschal victim, paschal bread;
> with sincerity and love
> eat we manna from above.
>
> Living God, who all life gives,
> Savior, by whose death we live,
> Spirit, guide through all our days:
> Three in One, your name we praise.
>
> [LATIN (1631), TRANS. ROBERT CAMPBELL (1849), ALT.]

TAKING THE BREAD AND CUP

THE GREAT THANKSGIVING
(see denominational resources, for example UMBOW, p. 66)

THE LORD'S PRAYER

BREAKING THE BREAD

GIVING THE BREAD AND CUP

PRAYER OF THANKSGIVING
We give glory to you, Lord, who raised up your cross to span the jaws of death like a bridge by which souls might pass from the region of the dead to the land of the living. You are incontestably alive. Your murderers sowed your living body in the earth as farmers sow grain, but it sprang up and yielded an abundant harvest of all those raised from the dead.

[ADAPTED FROM A PRAYER OF EPHREM THE SYRIAN, 4TH C.; DTB]

To you be all praise and glory! Thanks be to God!!

DISMISSAL WITH BLESSING
Now may the God of peace who brought back from the dead our Lord Jesus, the great shepherd of the sheep, by the blood of the eternal covenant, make you complete in everything good so that you may do

his will, working among us that which is pleasing in his sight, through Jesus Christ, to whom be the glory forever and ever!
Amen! Alleluia!

(Hebrews 13:20-21)

HYMN [77.77 D; Tune: EASTER HYMN, *UMH* 302]

Christ the Lord is risen today, Alleluia!
Earth and heaven in chorus say, Alleluia!
Raise your joys and triumphs high, Alleluia!
Sing, ye heavens, and earth reply, Alleluia!

Love's redeeming work is done, Alleluia!
Fought the fight, the battle won, Alleluia!
Death in vain forbids him rise, Alleluia!
Christ has opened paradise, Alleluia!

Lives again our glorious King, Alleluia!
Where, O death, is now thy sting? Alleluia!
Once he died our souls to save, Alleluia!
Where's thy victory, boasting grave? Alleluia!

Soar we now where Christ has led, Alleluia!
Following our exalted Head, Alleluia!
Made like him, like him we rise, Alleluia!
Ours the cross, the grave, the skies, Alleluia!

[CHARLES WESLEY, 1739]